Preference-Based Teaching
*Helping People With Developmental Disabilities
Enjoy Learning Without Problem Behavior*

Dennis H. Reid and Carolyn W. Green

*Volume II
In
The Behavior Analysis Applications
In Developmental Disabilities Series*

Habilitative Management Consultants, Inc.

Copyright © 2005 by Dennis H. Reid
All Rights Reserved

This book may not be reproduced or transmitted in any form or by any means, electronic, mechanical, including photocopying, recording, or by any information storage and retrieval system, except in the case of reviews, without the expressed written permission of the publisher, except where permitted by law.

ISBN Number 0-9645562-4-3

Published by
Habilitative Management Consultants, Inc.
P. O. Box 2295
Morganton, North Carolina 28680

Acknowledgements

We have been fortunate to work with many competent people in our research and practice in developing the procedures that constitute *preference-based teaching*. However, there are several individuals who have worked most closely with one or both of us specifically in investigating evidence-based procedures for increasing independence and/or enjoyment among people with developmental disabilities. We offer our sincere gratitude to these colleagues: Marsha Parsons, Perry Lattimore, Maureen Schepis, Leah Brackett, and Jeannia Rollyson.

About The Authors

Dr. Dennis Reid and Dr. Carolyn Green have worked in the human services for over 25 years. They have been involved in teaching services for people with developmental disabilities in homes, schools, residential centers, vocational sites, group homes, supported living and employment settings, and adult day programs. Denny and Carolyn have provided consultative and training services in over 30 states, and collectively have published over 100 journal articles and book chapters related to teaching services for individuals with developmental disabilities. Their work has resulted in awards and recognition from local, state, and national organizations, including the American Association on Mental Retardation, Association for Behavior Analysis, and TASH (formerly The Association for Persons With Severe Handicaps). Denny is currently the Director of the Carolina Behavior Analysis and Support Center in Morganton, North Carolina, and Carolyn is Director of Rosewood Resource Center, also in Morganton.

To Contact The Authors

Requests for consultative and training services from Denny Reid and Carolyn Green should be directed to the address below. Readers are also invited to send comments about this book, as well as ideas for future editions in the *Behavior Analysis Applications in Developmental Disabilities Series*.

Habilitative Management Consultants, Inc.
P. O. Box 2295
Morganton, North Carolina 28680
e-mail: drhmc@vistatech.net

CONTENTS

SECTION I

Introduction

Chapter 1 Introduction to *Preference-Based Teaching* 3
- A Technology of Teaching
- Purpose of *Preference-Based Teaching*
- Intended Audience of *Preference-Based Teaching*
- Focus of *Preference-Based Teaching*
- Organization of *Preference-Based Teaching*
- Explanation of Terms
- Chapter Review Questions

Chapter 2 An Evidence-Based Approach to Making Teaching Enjoyable for Learners with Disabilities 15
- What Happens When Evidence-Based Procedures Are Not Used
- How to Determine if An Evidence Base Exists
- Chapter Review Questions

SECTION II

Pre-Requisites for Making Teaching Enjoyable

Chapter 3 Ensuring Effective Teaching 25
- The *Teaching Skills Program*
- Qualification: Teaching New Skills Versus

Requiring Compliance
- Chapter Review Questions

Chapter 4 Teaching for *Functional* Skill Development 43
- Concern Regarding the Types of Skills Programs are Designed to Teach
- Guidelines for Determining Functional Skills for Teaching Programs Involving Teenagers and Adults
- Chapter Review Questions

SECTION III

The Specifics for Making Teaching Enjoyable

Chapter 5 Developing a Good Teacher-Learner Relationship 59
- Difficulties Encountered When a Good Teacher-Learner Relationship Does Not Exist
- Why a Good Teacher-Learner Relationship is Not Always Developed
- How to Develop a Good Teacher-Learner Relationship
- Overcoming Common Obstacles to Establishing A Good Teacher-Learner Relationship
- Chapter Review Questions

Chapter 6 Organizing A Teaching Session For Learner Enjoyment: The *Preferred Antecedent, Behavior, Consequence Model* 75
- Conducting Enjoyable Antecedent Activities
- Enjoyable Activities Associated with Teacher and Learner Behavior During a Teaching Session
- Conducting Enjoyable Activities As a Consequence To A Teaching Session
- Chapter Review Questions

Chapter 7 Building Choice Into Teaching Programs 91
- Providing Choice-Making Opportunities in Accordance with a Learner's Skill Level
- Special Considerations in Determining a Choice-

- Presentation Strategy
- Providing Choices as Antecedents and Consequences To a Teaching Session
- Chapter Review Questions

Chapter 8 Positive Reinforcers and Preferred Events 105
- A Review of Providing Reinforcement During Teaching
- Providing Preferred Events
- Ways to Identify Learner Preferences
- Ensuring Preferred Items and Activities are Presented As Part of The Teaching Process
- Chapter Review Questions

Chapter 9 The Timing of Teaching: Considerations For When To Conduct Teaching Sessions 117
- Guidelines for The Timing of Teaching Sessions
- Chapter Review Questions

SECTION IV

Keeping Teaching Enjoyable

Chapter 10 Enhancing Teacher Enjoyment 133
- Increase Learner Enjoyment with Teaching Programs
- Supplement Teaching Programs with Naturalistic Teaching
- Self-Motivation for Teachers
- Secure Support from Others
- Chapter Review Questions

Chapter 11 Supervisory Responsibilities For Supporting Teaching Effectiveness and Enjoyment 145
- Espousing Agency Values that Support Learner Skill Acquisition and Enjoyment
- Setting the Occasion for Effective and Enjoyable Teaching
- Responding in Ways That Support Effective and Enjoyable Teaching

- Chapter Review Questions

SECTION V

Bringing It All Together and Trouble Shooting

Chapter 12 A Checklist for *Preference-Based Teaching* 159

Chapter 13 Frequently Asked Questions About *Preference-Based Teaching* 163

SECTION VI

Selected Readings 169

Appendices 177
    Appendix A: Research Investigations that Developed and Validated Procedures Used in *Preference-Based Teaching*
    Appendix B: *The Teaching Skills Program*
    Appendix C: Instructions for Evaluating and Completing the Checklist for Teaching Proficiency

Index 183

Section I
Introduction

Chapter 1

Introduction to *Preference-Based Teaching*

A major responsibility of support personnel in the developmental disabilities field is helping individuals learn meaningful skills. All people with developmental disabilities, and most notably those who have mental retardation or autism, experience difficulties with learning. Most individuals will not overcome their learning difficulties unless they receive effective teaching services from support persons.

Teaching meaningful skills is necessary for individuals with disabilities to maximize their independence and experience a lifestyle they prefer and enjoy. Teaching meaningful skills is also the most efficacious means of preventing problem behavior that is displayed by a number of people with developmental disabilities.

Perhaps most importantly, teaching useful skills allows individuals with developmental disabilities to exert control over their lives. Individual control and freedom is a cherished value among all people, whether they have disabilities or not. To have control over one's life, a person must have the skills to function independently and to satisfy personal needs in ways the individual desires. Unless people with developmental disabilities are directly taught meaningful skills to promote independence, their lives will be controlled in large part by other people.

> **Effective teaching is a basic necessity for giving people with developmental disabilities control over their lives.**

A Technology for Teaching

Since the 1960s, extensive research and application have resulted in an amazingly effective technology for teaching people who have developmental disabilities. Grounded in the principles and practices of applied behavior analysis, this technology repeatedly has helped people with even the most significant disabilities learn a wide array of useful skills. Initial applications of the technology helped people with severe and profound mental retardation learn basic self-help skills such as eating and toileting that, prior to the 1960s, were considered impossible for this population to learn. Since the early successes, the teaching technology has helped people with all levels of disabilities acquire meaningful skills in every major life domain. In short, there is a very effective technology of teaching for assisting people with developmental disabilities to acquire skills needed to live increasingly independent and enjoyable lives, and to have significant control over their lives.

Problems Applying the Teaching Technology

Despite the noted successes of behavior analytic teaching procedures, application of the technology has encountered obstacles. One obstacle that is especially troublesome, and particularly from the perspective of people with disabilities who are recipients of teaching services, is that *participating in teaching programs can be effortful and unpleasant*. People with developmental disabilities often do not like to participate in teaching programs.

Anyone who is experienced in teaching people with developmental disabilities has likely encountered difficulties due to a respective individual not enjoying a teaching program. Such dislike is reflected in many ways. When individuals do not enjoy an ongoing teaching program, they are likely to show their displeasure by:

- **Refusing to begin scheduled teaching sessions**
- **Refusing to do anything during teaching sessions**
- **Aggressing toward whomever is trying to teach them**
- **Destroying teaching materials during a teaching session**
- **Complaining, crying, or showing other signs of discomfort or distress**
- **Biting their wrists or other forms of self-injurious behavior**

The negative effects of an individual not liking a given teaching program as just illustrated will be discussed more in-depth in **Chapter 2**.

On a general level, such dislike is a primary reason many people with developmental disabilities do not receive the teaching services they need to develop meaningful skills. When individuals do not like participating in teaching programs, the programs often are discontinued prematurely, or are not conducted in the manner in which they are designed to be conducted. Consequently, programs lose their effectiveness in helping individuals learn useful skills. In other cases, teaching programs are provided despite the apparent displeasure of the participating learner. In the latter situations, participation in teaching programs represents an unpleasant and often dreaded part of the day for people with disabilities.

Overcoming Dislike of Teaching Programs:
Making Teaching Enjoyable

In some ways, discontent associated with participating in teaching programs might be expected. Learning new skills often requires effort on the part of the person being taught, as well as a considerable amount of practice. Exerting effort and repeatedly trying to do something can be unpleasant for anyone. Many teaching programs, and particularly for people who have more severe disabilities, also require physical prompting in which the individual is physically guided through various movements by the person doing the teaching. Being touched and physically guided in a repeated fashion can also be unpleasant for many people.

There are other aspects of teaching procedures that inherently involve practices that tend to be disliked. These will be discussed in subsequent chapters. However, the primary reasons that participation in teaching programs is often unpleasant for people with developmental disabilities have more to do with *how* the teaching procedures are carried out rather than the teaching procedures themselves. Even procedures such as physical prompting that may be inherently unpleasant for individuals can be conducted in ways that make the teaching process much more desirable.

Providing teaching programs in ways individuals find enjoyable has only recently received the attention of the behavior analytic field that developed the technology of teaching for people with developmental disabilities. Nonetheless, that attention has quickly resulted in a substantial amount of knowledge about how to make teaching enjoyable. It also has become increasingly apparent that if people with developmental disabilities are to benefit more significantly from the available teaching technology, that technology must be applied in a way that individuals enjoy.

> **Teaching should be conducted in an enjoyable manner such that individuals with disabilities like to participate in teaching programs.**

Purpose of *Preference-Based Teaching*

The purpose of **Preference-Based Teaching** is to describe how to make teaching programs enjoyable for people who have developmental disabilities. The intent is to assist support personnel in applying effective teaching procedures in ways that individuals with disabilities truly enjoy. Numerous strategies will be described such that a teaching program can be designed and carried out in a way that is specifically tailored to an individual's unique preferences. Using procedures described throughout this book, teaching programs can be provided such that individuals with disabilities *look forward* to teaching sessions; participating in teaching programs becomes a desired and pleasantly anticipated event.

The procedures to be described for making teaching enjoyable represent a *preference-based* approach to teaching. Individual preferences of people with disabilities are embedded within the teaching process. Conducting teaching sessions in association with preferred items, activities, and situations makes the overall teaching process much more enjoyable for recipients of the teaching services relative to traditional teaching approaches.

Intended Audience of *Preference-Based Teaching*

The primary audience of **Preference-Based Teaching** is anyone who develops and/or carries out teaching programs with people who have developmental disabilities. The content is especially directed to:

- **classroom teachers**
- **teacher assistants**
- **residential support staff**
- **job coaches**
- **adult day activity staff**

- **sheltered workshop staff**

The content of ***Preference-Based Teaching*** is also designed for parents who desire to carry out teaching programs in a way that not only leads to important skill development, but represents an enjoyable experience for their sons and daughters. The content likewise should be most useful for those who train others how to teach, such as special education professors as well as staff development personnel in human service agencies.

Focus of *Preference-Based Teaching*

Focus on People Who Have Severe Disabilities

Ways of making teaching enjoyable that will be described throughout this text are applicable for people with any type of developmental disability. Whether a person has mental retardation or autism, mild or profound disabilities, various procedures can be tailored to the specific preferences of the individual. However, a special focus will be on people who have *severe* disabilities. The latter individuals may have severe or profound cognitive disabilities, autism, or multiple disabilities.

The focus on people who have severe disabilities exists for two reasons. First, due to the severity of their disabilities, these individuals usually require more time to learn meaningful skills. Correspondingly, people with severe disabilities must participate in teaching programs for greater periods of time relative to people who have less serious disabilities. Generally, the longer a teaching program must be conducted, the more likely participation in the program will become unpleasant. Increased likelihood of unpleasantness occurs because of increased effort on the part of the person being taught. The more often a teaching program is carried out, the more practice and effort is required to try to perform the skills being taught.

Teaching programs that take longer to conduct, or require more learning trials, also can become unpleasant for the person doing the teaching. The latter situation develops because repeatedly carrying out a teaching program becomes increasingly effortful. Many people who attempt to teach a skill to an individual with a developmental disability over days, weeks, and even months become frustrated or otherwise tired of carrying out the teaching program. The general unpleasantness associated with repeatedly carrying out a teaching program also has a negative effect on the person being taught. In essence, the displeasure encountered in conducting a teaching program carries over to the recipient of the program. An unpleasant cycle subsequently develops in which discontent among the person carrying out the teaching program and the individual being taught continuously escalates displeasure between the teacher and learner.

> **If teaching is unpleasant for the person doing the teaching, the teaching process invariably becomes disliked by the person being taught.**

The second reason our focus is on individuals with severe disabilities is that teaching procedures for this population often involve more components likely to be unpleasant relative to procedures applied with people who have less significant disabilities. For example, teaching people with severe disabilities often requires more emphasis on physical prompting strategies. As noted previously, many individuals do not enjoy being physically guided by another person. People especially do not like to be physically guided repeatedly, which is often a necessary part of teaching programs with persons who have severe disabilities.

As also indicated earlier, procedures that make teaching programs enjoyable for individuals with severe disabilities can be incorporated within programs for people with less serious disabilities. However, specifically how the procedures are applied with the latter individuals may need to be altered. How various procedures can be applied in somewhat different ways for people with less significant disabilities will be highlighted periodically throughout remaining chapters.

Although an emphasis will be on people who have severe disabilities, there is no qualification regarding ages of individuals. The procedures for making teaching enjoyable to be discussed can be applied with all age groups of people with developmental disabilities, from toddlers in early intervention settings to senior citizens in retirement living or recreational situations.

Focus on Formal Teaching Programs and Sessions

Teaching people with developmental disabilities can be conducted in a number of ways. The focus here though is on what is generally considered to be *formal teaching programs* and *formal teaching sessions*.

Formal teaching programs refer to specifically prepared plans for teaching a respective skill to an individual. These plans usually contain a number of specific components, such as a task analysis of the skill to be learned into a series of discrete steps or behaviors, and a heavy reliance on data to evaluate learning progress and make teaching refinements. Formal teaching programs often constitute integral parts of overall service plans, such as Individual Education Plans (IEPs) in schools, Individual Family Service Plans in preschool and early intervention settings, and Individual Program, Habilitative, or Person-Centered Plans in residential and adult day-treatment settings.

Formal teaching sessions refer to teaching that is conducted in a situation that is somewhat separate from the ongoing daily routine. A teacher, staff person, or parent works individually with a learner for the sole purpose of carrying out a formal teaching program. A common example is when a teacher sits down with a student at a table to carry out an individualized teaching program that is part of the student's IEP while other personnel work with remaining students in the classroom. As such, the teaching is conducted during a circumscribed period of time, and often in a set location.

Formal teaching programs and sessions are emphasized in regard to making teaching enjoyable because this approach is often the most common teaching format in typical settings for people with severe disabilities. Additionally, although necessary for substantial learning to occur among people with severe disabilities, formal teaching programs and sessions often encounter the most difficulties with teaching being disliked by participating individuals. Less formal approaches to teaching, which are also important to the overall learning process for people with severe disabilities, generally present fewer problems with respect to the teaching being enjoyable. The latter teaching formats should supplement formal teaching approaches. Opportune times and situations for conducting informal teaching procedures, and ways to maximize enjoyment within those processes, will be discussed in relevant parts of subsequent chapters (see in particular *naturalistic teaching approaches* in **Chapter 10**).

Focus on Evidence-Based Procedures

A final focus of **Preference-Based Teaching** is on *evidence-based* ways to make teaching enjoyable. Evidence-based refers to procedures that have been tried and tested through scientific research to substantiate the procedures' effectiveness. Although many of the procedures to be discussed have been drawn from our experience, the procedures nevertheless stem from applied behavior analytic research that has substantiated the basis for the procedures. Adhering to procedures developed and validated through applied research increases the likelihood the procedures will effectively increase individual enjoyment with the teaching process. Such adherence also decreases the likelihood that procedures will be used that have little probability of success, even though the procedures may be popular. Elaboration on the evidence base of the procedures to be described throughout this book, and problems likely to arise if evidence-based procedures are not employed, is provided in **Chapter 2**.

Organization of *Preference-Based Teaching*

Preference-Based Teaching is organized into six sections. Readers can go directly to a respective section that addresses a topic of the most interest. However, for maximum utility it is recommended that at some point the sections be read in their existing sequence.

Section I: Introduction

Section I introduces *Preference-Based Teaching* through the current chapter. Subsequently, **Chapter 2** describes the importance of relying on evidence-based procedures to ensure teaching is both effective and enjoyable for the learner. The latter chapter also describes what constitutes an acceptable evidence base, and likely pitfalls encountered if approaches to teaching are used that do not have a sound basis in scientific evidence.

Section II: Pre-Requisites for Making Teaching Enjoyable

Making teaching enjoyable for people with disabilities will be of limited value if the teaching programs are not effective; the programs must result in individuals acquiring the skills that are the focus of the teaching. **Chapter 3** in this section summarizes basic components that are necessary for teaching programs to be successful. Because only a summary is presented, this chapter also provides the interested reader with important references to other available sources for more in-depth discussions on effective teaching procedures for people with developmental disabilities.

In addition to being effective in terms of individuals acquiring the skills being taught, teaching programs must focus on skills that are truly meaningful for people with developmental disabilities. A pervasive problem with formal teaching programs, and particularly for older individuals who have severe disabilities, is the programs do not focus on skills that have any significant impact on individuals learning to live more independently or enjoyably. For a variety of reasons as will be discussed later, teaching programs often focus on skills that are convenient to teach but are quite irrelevant for assisting individuals with disabilities in learning anything useful. **Chapter 4** presents several well-established guidelines for ensuring that what is selected to be taught to individuals with disabilities has true meaning for the individuals.

Section III: The Specifics for Making Teaching Enjoyable

This section, consisting of five chapters, describes specific procedures for making teaching enjoyable for people who have developmental disabilities. **Chapter 5** focuses on what is arguably the most critical factor affecting individual enjoyment with the teaching process: the existing relationship between the person doing the teaching and the recipient of the teaching program. This chapter presents specific ways to establish a desirable relationship with each individual who will participate in a teaching program. **Chapter 6** describes a general approach for organizing teaching sessions in order to make the process enjoyable. Organizing teaching sessions pertains to what is done before, during, and after a teaching session. **Chapters 7**, **8**, and **9** then describe specific activities that can be conducted before, during, and after teaching sessions to make the overall process enjoyable. Respective topics to be covered include providing choices, positive reinforcers and generally pleasant events, and the timing of when teaching sessions should and should not be conducted.

Section IV: Keeping Teaching Enjoyable

As referred to earlier, teaching programs for people with severe disabilities often must be carried out for relatively extended time periods. As also noted, the longer a teaching program is carried out, the more likely the program will become unpleasant for the participant. The chapters in this section focus on how to keep a teaching program enjoyable over the long run. **Chapter 10** describes what can be done to make sure the teaching process is an enjoyable activity for people who carry out teaching programs (which again, is necessary to help the process continue to be enjoyable for the person being taught). **Chapter 11** addresses what supervisors in agencies providing teaching services should do to help agency personnel experience enjoyment and success with their teaching responsibilities.

Section V: Bringing It All Together and Trouble Shooting

Chapter 12 incorporates information described in preceding chapters into a step-by-step checklist of how to make teaching enjoyable. The checklist can be used prior to initiating a formal teaching session to ensure everything reasonable has been built into the process to maximize learner enjoyment. Subsequently, **Chapter 13** focuses on preventing and resolving common problems with making teaching enjoyable by addressing *Frequently Asked Questions.* The questions and corresponding responses stem from experiences of people who have encountered problems with teaching being disliked by respective individuals with developmental disabilities.

Section VI: Selected Readings and Appendices

In the **Selected Readings** and **Appendices**, numerous sources of additional information are provided that pertain to making teaching enjoyable and effective for people with developmental disabilities. Respective chapters refer to **Selected Readings** and **Appendices** providing resource material relevant to topics covered in the chapters.

Chapter Review Questions

All chapters except **12** (the *Preference-Based Teaching Checklist*) and **13** (*Frequently Asked Questions*) conclude with short-answer review questions. The questions are designed to enhance the reader's acquisition and subsequent application of information covered in respective chapters. The review questions are also intended to assist readers who desire to train other people in ways to make teaching enjoyable for people who have developmental disabilities.

Explanation of Terms

People who are responsible for implementing teaching programs for people with developmental disabilities fill many roles and have many titles. For clarification and simplicity, we will refer to these people simply as *teachers*. The term "teacher" is used in a functional sense throughout this text to refer to anyone carrying out a teaching program with an individual who has a developmental disability.

Our reference to teachers in the manner just noted should not be interpreted as a discredit to *professional* teachers – personnel who have received undergraduate or graduate training and licensure as a teacher within a school system. People with specialized training and licensing to teach within school systems obviously represent a valued and highly important source of service for individuals with developmental disabilities. Professional teachers are likewise a primary audience of this book. Our inclusion of other support personnel (see previous description of **Intended Audience**) under the general descriptor of "teacher" is designed only for simplicity of presentation. The intent is to provide the procedures for making teaching enjoyable available for anyone who has responsibility for carrying out teaching programs, even if they have not had extensive training in teaching procedures.

- **Teacher: Anyone carrying out a teaching program**

Also for clarification and simplicity of presentation, we will refer to people with disabilities who are the recipients of teaching programs as *learners*. As with references to teachers, our reference to learners is used in a functional sense. Teaching programs are designed to help people learn, whether the programs are carried out in school classrooms, group homes, supported work sites, homes, or any other location in which people with disabilities spend their time. When such programs are carried out effectively, the participants with developmental disabilities will indeed be learners.

- **Learner: Person with a developmental disability who is being taught**

Chapter Review Questions

1. *What are three reasons why it is important to teach meaningful skills to people who have developmental disabilities?*

2. *What is the relationship between people with developmental disabilities being taught meaningful skills and personal control?*

3. *What is a major obstacle in using common behavioral teaching procedures for helping people with developmental disabilities learn new skills?*

4. *How does learner enjoyment relate to the success of teaching programs?*

Chapter 2

An Evidence-Based Approach to Making Teaching Enjoyable for Learners with Disabilities

The technology of teaching that has assisted many people with developmental disabilities in learning useful skills is the result of years of research devoted to developing and refining the technology. Literally hundreds of applied behavior analytic studies have been conducted to develop the technology, and to ensure the teaching procedures truly help people with disabilities learn new skills. Such research provides a strong evidence base to support the efficacy of the teaching procedures that are currently available.

Having an evidence base that demonstrates procedural effectiveness is likewise important when considering ways to make teaching enjoyable for learners. When support personnel and family members want to help an individual with developmental disabilities enjoy learning, they should have access to procedures proven to be effective through sound research. Although the research attention directed to making teaching enjoyable has been less than that directed to developing teaching procedures in general, the research that has been conducted is highly relevant. That research provides the evidence base for enhancing the likelihood that procedures designed to make teaching enjoyable for people with developmental disabilities will indeed be successful.

What Happens When Evidence-Based Procedures Are Not Used

If evidence-based procedures are not used when attempting to make teaching programs enjoyable for people with developmental disabilities, numerous problems arise. Most apparently, the likelihood that the approaches will actually help learners enjoy participating in the teaching process decreases significantly. When there is no evidence base to support the design of the procedures, making teaching enjoyable often becomes guess work. Some guesses may actually turn out to be successful, but many will not. Teachers frequently will be relying on procedures that even though well intended, have little or no impact on learner enjoyment with the teaching process.

> **When attempts to make teaching enjoyable are based on procedures that have no scientific evidence to support their effectiveness, it is unlikely the procedures will have a consistent impact on learner enjoyment.**

Unsuccessful attempts to make teaching enjoyable often result in one or more of the problems noted in **Chapter 1** that occur when learners do not like participating in a teaching program. To review briefly, when learners are not enjoying the teaching process, they are likely to:

- **Refuse to begin scheduled teaching sessions**
- **Refuse to do anything during teaching sessions**
- **Aggress toward whomever is trying to teach**
- **Destroy teaching materials during teaching sessions**
- **Complain, cry, or show other signs of discomfort or distress**
- **Bite their wrists or other forms of self-injurious behavior**

As also noted in **Chapter 1**, when a learner does not like to participate in a teaching program, the teaching process invariably becomes unpleasant for the teacher. Subsequently, the teacher tends to avoid carrying out the program, hurries through the teaching, or carries out only part of the teaching program. As a result, the teaching program is not implemented in the intended manner and is not only disliked by the learner, but is not likely to represent effective teaching.

Even if a teacher persists in carrying out a teaching program when a learner does not enjoy the teaching process, the teaching is not likely to help the learner acquire new skills. Negative reactions on the part of the learner due to discontent with the program frequently force the teacher to alter the teaching program. Teachers often change or omit parts of instructional programs to reduce resistive behavior by the learner, or to avoid learner resistance altogether. Again, when teaching programs are altered such that instructional procedures are not conducted in the manner in which they were designed, programs lose their effectiveness for teaching new skills.

Another result of a teacher persisting in carrying out a teaching program that a learner dislikes was noted in **Chapter 1**: the teaching session becomes an unpleasant and even dreaded part of the learner's day. Participating in these types of teaching sessions seriously detracts from day-to-day quality of life among people who have developmental disabilities.

In light of the problems associated with carrying out teaching programs that people with disabilities do not like, questions arise as to why teachers would persist with such programs. In many cases, teachers persist because they know the importance of teaching useful skills to people with disabilities. Teachers sometimes adopt the attitude that teaching is important for the well-being of their learners even if the process is not something the learners enjoy. Teachers reason that everybody has to do some things that are disliked in order to better themselves; in this case, a learner participating in a teaching program that is disliked. Such reasoning is understandable and even admirable in some cases. Nonetheless, the impact on the learner's skill acquisition and overall quality of life is almost always compromised.

In other cases, support personnel persist with teaching programs that are disliked not because of the importance they place on teaching, but because they are concerned about what will happen if they do not carry out assigned teaching duties. Teachers in special education and related school programs must carry out teaching programs to maintain their jobs, or at least to avoid the wrath of their principals or related personnel. In other situations, such as Intermediate Care Facilities funded under the Federal Title XIX Medicaid program, teaching must occur to maintain agency funding. Staff charged with implementing teaching programs in the latter agencies can receive harsh criticism or disciplinary action if it becomes apparent that teaching programs are not being carried out as scheduled.

Problems associated with teaching programs disliked by learners can be resolved if procedures to enhance learner enjoyment that have a strong evidence base to support their efficacy are incorporated within the programs. Teachers should have ready access to evidence-based procedures that make teaching programs both effective and enjoyable.

How To Determine If An Evidence Base Exists

The importance of evidence-based procedures derived from applied research as part of teaching and related practices is receiving increased attention. Family members are becoming increasingly concerned about their sons and daughters with developmental disabilities receiving services that are well liked and effective. Society in general is also expecting more accountability from the education and human service sectors.

For schools and other agencies providing teaching services, accountability means that their teaching services clearly result in individuals with developmental disabilities learning useful skills, and are well received by learners. If individuals are to learn and respond favorably to teaching services then the procedures applied by teachers must be effective and enjoyable. Again, teaching procedures are more likely to be effective and enjoyable if the procedures have scientific evidence to support their efficacy and enjoyment capacity.

Increased concern over reliance on evidence-based teaching procedures and accountability in general is also due to growing recognition that many teaching services are not very effective, nor very well received by learners. To illustrate, individuals with developmental disabilities often spend months and even years participating in a teaching program without mastering the skills the program is designed to teach. A primary reason many approaches to teaching are not effective is that the component teaching procedures do not have an empirically substantiated evidence base. Rather, many support personnel rely on approaches to teaching that are based on current fads, folklore, or guess work. Other approaches are used that although traditionally espoused by the professional field, have never been adequately researched to validate their effectiveness.

Educational services for people with developmental disabilities as well as human services in general involve a number of ineffective and in some cases, detrimental practices. Such practices are frequently well intended, but nevertheless result in little success in terms of people with disabilities learning useful skills. In some cases, professionals desire to disseminate effective approaches to teaching as a means of helping teachers and other support personnel, but do not invest the time to adequately research their recommended approaches. In other cases, professionals sincerely believe what they have to offer persons charged with teaching responsibilities will represent effective teaching practices, and see no need to research their recommendations. In either case, the result is the same: teaching procedures are disseminated and adopted that have no scientific basis to support their utility.

> **A primary reason many educational practices with people who have developmental disabilities are ineffective is that the practices are adopted with no scientific evidence base to support their efficacy.**

Responsible teaching requires teachers to use procedures that are likely to be effective. It is incumbent upon teachers to seek and apply teaching practices that have an evidence base to support their efficacy. In defense of teachers who routinely rely on teaching-related practices without a sound scientific base though, it can be difficult to determine if an evidence base exists for recommended practices. Again, agencies providing teaching services for people with developmental disabilities are frequently inundated with recommended approaches to teaching, regardless of any evidence base to substantiate the recommendations.

It is beyond the scope of this text to thoroughly describe what constitutes a scientifically acceptable evidence base for teaching-related practices. However, the basic components of necessary research warrant mention. For teaching-related procedures to be considered to have an evidence base grounded in scientific research, the procedures must at least be shown under conditions of scientific control to result in:

- **A learner demonstrating a designated skill that the learner could not perform prior to receiving the procedure (i.e., the learner acquiring the skill)**

- **Different learners acquiring the skill in a variety of different situations**

- **Learners acquiring skills when different teachers use the same procedures**

Although there are many more aspects to scientifically validating the effectiveness of teaching practices, the three just noted features are the most basic. These features are likewise relevant when considering procedures specifically designed for making teaching enjoyable for people who have developmental disabilities. A recommended procedure for making a teaching program enjoyable should have been shown within acceptable parameters of scientific control to result in:

- **Increased enjoyment for a given learner when the procedure is incorporated within a teaching program**

- **Increased enjoyment for other learners when the procedure is applied**

- **Increased enjoyment for other learners when the procedure is applied by other teachers**

When procedures designed for making teaching enjoyable meet these criteria, then generally the procedures can be considered to have a strong evidence base to support their effectiveness. As such, the likelihood that the procedures will be successful when applied as part of subsequent teaching practices is enhanced immeasurably.

As highlighted in **Chapter 1**, the procedures to be presented in the remaining chapters for making teaching enjoyable have an evidence base in scientific research as just summarized. For readers interested in more information about the research foundation of the procedures, **Appendix A** provides references to a number of the key investigations upon which the procedures to be discussed are based.

Chapter Review Questions

1. *What is the major problem encountered when evidence-based procedures are not used in attempts to enhance learner enjoyment with teaching programs?*

2. *What are two negative effects of a teacher persisting in carrying out a teaching program that a learner dislikes?*

3. *What is a primary reason that many educational practices with people who have developmental disabilities are ineffective?*

4. *What three conditions must be met if a recommended procedure for making a teaching program enjoyable is to be considered to have a scientific evidence base to support the procedure's efficacy?*

Section II
Pre-Requisites for Making Teaching Enjoyable

Chapter 3

Ensuring Effective Teaching

As emphasized in preceding chapters, teaching programs must be conducted in an effective manner. There is no justifiable reason to involve people with developmental disabilities in teaching programs if the programs do not effectively assist the individuals in learning new skills. As also stressed previously, despite the availability of a highly effective technology of teaching, in practice many teaching programs are not very effective. A quick review of teaching programs that constitute IEPs, habilitation plans, etc., will reveal the same teaching programs in existence from year to year for a given individual. The teaching programs continue to exist because despite their implementation during the preceding year, individual learners did not acquire the skills targeted by the programs.

There are a number of reasons why many teaching programs are not effective with people who have developmental disabilities. However, there are two most common reasons:

- **Teaching programs are not designed adequately to incorporate components of the available teaching technology**

- **Teaching programs are not carried out in the way the programs are intended to be implemented**

These two reasons underscore the importance of ensuring the design and implementation of teaching programs coincide with what research has shown to represent effective teaching practices. People with developmental disabilities will not benefit very much from teaching programs if the existing evidence-based technology of teaching is not adhered to in the design and implementation of the programs.

In light of problems encountered with the effectiveness of many teaching programs, attention is warranted to ensure teaching programs are appropriately designed and implemented. Although the emphasis of this text is on how to make teaching enjoyable, the benefit of building enjoyment into teaching programs will be limited if the programs do not result in people with developmental disabilities learning useful skills. Correspondingly, before focusing on how to make teaching enjoyable for learners with disabilities, attention is directed to ensuring that teaching programs are indeed effective.

This chapter summarizes the essential components of an effective teaching program for people who have developmental disabilities. An approach to teaching will be described that has a solid evidence base to support its efficacy. The teaching approach to be presented is also practical in that it can be readily applied in typical settings in which teaching is conducted with people who have developmental disabilities.

The *Teaching Skills Program*

The approach to teaching to be described is the **Teaching Skills Program**. This program was designed specifically for effectiveness and practicality in settings providing teaching services for people with developmental disabilities. The **Teaching Skills Program** was also designed so that support personnel who have teaching responsibilities could quickly learn to use the program.

In accordance with our emphasis on evidence-based teaching practices, the **Teaching Skills Program** has been researched repeatedly to develop and substantiate its effectiveness. The program has been shown to successfully teach skills to people with varying degrees of disabilities, including individuals with the most profound, multiple disabilities. Research has likewise demonstrated that teachers in residential and day treatment settings (including, for example, schools, workshops, adult activity programs, and supported work sites) can learn to apply the program effectively with less than one day of training in the program's component procedures. A sample of the research investigations that have resulted in the supporting evidence base of the **Teaching Skills Program's** effectiveness is provided in the following table.

Research that Developed and Substantiated the Effectiveness Of Teaching Procedures in the *Teaching Skills Program*

Schepis, M. M., Reid, D. H., Ownby, J., & Parsons, M. B. (2001). Training support staff to embed teaching within natural routines of young children with disabilities in an inclusive preschool. *Journal of Applied Behavior Analysis, 34,* 313-328.

Schepis, M. M., Ownby, J. B., Parsons, M. B., & Reid, D. H. (2000). Training support staff to teach young children with disabilities in an inclusive preschool setting. *Journal of Positive Behavior Interventions, 2,* 170-178.

Parsons, M. B., Reid, D. H., Green, C. W., & Browning, L. B. (1999). Reducing individualized job coach assistance provided to supported workers with multiple severe disabilities in supported work. *Journal of The Association for Persons With Severe Handicaps, 24,* 292-297.

Parsons, M. B., & Reid, D. H. (1999). Training basic teaching skills to paraeducators of students with severe disabilities: A one-day program. *Teaching Exceptional Children, 31,* 48-54.

Parsons, M. B., Reid, D. H., & Green, C. W. (1996). Training basic teaching skills to community and institutional support staff for people with severe disabilities: A one-day program. *Research in Developmental Disabilities, 17,* 467-485.

Parsons, M. B., Reid, D. H., & Green, C. W. (1993). Preparing direct service staff to teach people with severe disabilities: A comprehensive evaluation of an effective and acceptable training program. *Behavioral Residential Treatment, 8,* 163-186.

Parsons, M. B., & Reid, D. H. (1995). Training residential supervisors to provide feedback for maintaining staff teaching skills with people who have severe disabilities. *Journal of Applied Behavior Analysis, 28,* 95-96.

Before describing how the **Teaching Skills Program** can be used as an effective and practical way to teach important skills to people with developmental disabilities, it should be emphasized that this program represents only one approach to teaching. The technology of teaching consists of a wide array of teaching procedures, any number of which can be combined into an effective teaching program. We have selected this particular approach because again, it has a strong evidence base to support its efficacy and practicality. The **Teaching Skills Program** also represents an approach to teaching with which we are extremely familiar. We have been integrally involved in research that developed and evaluated the approach (see previous samples of investigations evaluating the program). We have likewise used the **Teaching Skills Program** repeatedly in our day-to-day work in teaching people with developmental disabilities, as well as in training other teachers to use the approach.

Although we support the **Teaching Skills Program** as a means for ensuring the effectiveness of teaching programs, our intent is not to deter readers from using other aspects of the technology of teaching developed through behavior analytic research and application. Teachers should use teaching procedures with which they are most comfortable, and that are best suited for their learners – provided that the procedures still represent appropriate application of evidence-based teaching strategies. The summary of the **Teaching Skills Program** provided in the remainder of this chapter is offered only as a model of how to apply aspects of the available teaching technology. For readers interested in other evidence-based approaches to teaching, a number of comprehensive texts are available that provide useful descriptions of teaching strategies. Some of the texts that we have found most useful are provided in the following table.

> **Useful Texts on Evidence-Based Teaching Strategies
> For People Who Have Developmental Disabilities**
>
> Alberto, P. A., & Troutman, A. C. (2002). *Applied behavior analysis for teachers* (6th edition). New York: Merrill.
>
> Snell, M. E., & Brown, F. (2000). *Instruction of students with severe disabilities* (5th edition). Upper Saddle River, NJ: Merrill/Prenctice Hall.
>
> Westling, D. L., & Fox, L. (2004). *Teaching students with severe disabilities* (3rd edition). Upper Saddle River, N.J.: Prentice Hall.
>
> Wolery, M., Ault, M. J., & Doyle, P. M. (1992). *Teaching students with moderate to severe disabilities: Use of response prompting strategies.* New York: Longman.

The **Teaching Skills Program** consists of four basic teaching components. These components include: (1) a *task analysis* of the skill being taught into the specific steps or behaviors that constitute the skill, (2) providing help or *prompting* the learner to perform the steps that the learner does not know how to perform, (3) *correcting errors* that the learner may display when attempting to perform a given step and, (4) supporting or *reinforcing* correct performance of the steps by the learner. Each of these components is summarized in subsequent chapter sections. For readers interested in more detail about the **Teaching Skills Program**, **Appendix B** provides information for obtaining the program in its entirety.

> **Basic Components of the Teaching Skills Program**
>
> 1. Task Analysis
> 2. Prompting
> 3. Error Correction
> 4. Reinforcement

Task Analysis

When teaching a new skill to a person with a developmental disability, it is usually necessary to break the skill down into the specific behaviors or steps that are needed to perform the skill. The process of breaking a skill into its component steps is accomplished through a *task analysis*. For example, when teaching a man with profound cognitive disabilities how to wipe his face with a napkin during mealtime, a task analysis of the face-wiping skill might consist of the steps of: (1) picking up the napkin, (2) wiping the mouth with the napkin and, (3) returning the napkin to the table.

Most skills targeted within teaching programs can be broken down into discrete behaviors by using a task analysis. The task analysis may involve many steps for more complex skills, or only a few steps for less complex skills (see following examples).

Example of a (Complex) Task Analysis for Preparing an Envelope To Mail a Book as Part of a Supported Work Task

Step #	Action
1.	pick up envelope off stack of envelopes
2.	place envelope face up on table
3.	pick up "return address" stamp
4.	place stamp on upper left corner of envelope
5.	put stamp on table
6.	pick up "media rate" stamp
7.	place stamp on envelope
8.	return stamp to table
9.	pick up book
10.	pick up envelope and orient with open end up
11.	place book in envelope
12.	pick up advertising flier
13.	place flier in envelope
14.	place completed envelope in "finished" box

Example of A (Simple) Task Analysis for Turning on a Television Using a Remote Control

Step #	Action
1.	pick up remote
2.	point remote toward television
3.	push "power" button

Using a task analysis to break a skill into its component steps has several advantages from a teaching perspective. First, the process makes it easier for an individual to learn to perform the skill because the learner can focus on one specific behavior at a time. Teaching is directed to helping the learner perform each step individually until all the steps can be performed in their sequence.

The second advantage of a task analysis is that by breaking a skill into specific behaviors, each of which occurs in sequence to perform the overall skill, it becomes easier for the learner to remember to perform each respective step. When each step is taught and practiced in sequence, each step becomes a cue or reminder for the learner regarding what should be done next in the skill sequence.

To illustrate, think of the fifth digit in your home telephone number. Most of us have to say to ourselves each digit in our telephone number in the appropriate sequence until we come to and identify the fifth digit. The reason we have to say each digit in sequence before we can identify the fifth digit is because when initially learning or memorizing our telephone number, we learned the digits in their exact order. In this manner, we essentially provided a task analysis of the telephone number into its constituent digits in their appropriate sequence. Each digit then became a cue or reminder for the next digit in the overall telephone number.

A third advantage of a task analysis is that when each step of a skill is identified – and typically written down – then it becomes more likely the skill will be taught in the same manner during each teaching session. Teaching the skill in the same manner across teaching sessions facilitates the learner's acquisition of the skill relative to sessions in which the skill is taught in different ways (e.g., different steps are taught or are taught in different sequences).

Using a task analysis to keep teaching sessions consistent is particularly important when different teachers carry out a teaching program with a given learner. Various personnel often are involved in conducting a teaching program with a learner in a number of settings. This is particularly the case in residential settings such as group homes in which there are different shifts of direct support staff. In these situations, one person might teach a learner on the day shift, a different staff member may teach the learner on the evening shift, and another staff person may teach the learner on the weekends. Unless there is a task analysis to guide the staffs' teaching, it is likely that the different staff will teach varying steps to the learner or teach the steps in varying sequences. If the latter process occurs and each staff member carries out a teaching program somewhat differently, it becomes more difficult for the learner to acquire the skill.

Advantages of a Task Analysis

Learning is facilitated by allowing
the learner to focus on one step at a time.

Learning becomes easier because each step in
the task helps remind the learner
what step to perform next.

The consistency of teaching
across teaching sessions is enhanced.

A task analysis can usually be developed by the teacher performing the skill and writing down each behavior required in sequence to complete the skill. The written behaviors or steps then form the task analysis that is used to guide what is taught to the learner. In the ***Teaching Skills Program***, task analyses are used such that during each teaching session, each step required to perform the entire skill is addressed with the learner in the exact sequence that the steps normally occur. That is, the *whole* skill is taught during each session by teaching each component step in its natural order.

Using a task analysis in the manner just summarized is the most common application of the task analysis component of the ***Teaching Skills Program***. However, there are certain situations in which a task analysis is not necessary. Most notably, some teaching programs for people who have the most significant disabilities involve only one step or behavior. For example, teaching a person with severe multiple disabilities to press a button on a device to activate a CD player may involve only one step (i.e., pressing the button). If a skill only involves one step, there is no need for a task analysis. Whether there is one or a number of steps comprising a given skill though, once identified the steps are then taught through the remaining components of the ***Teaching Skills Program***.

Prompting

When teaching a new skill to a person with a developmental disability, the individual typically needs help in performing various steps that comprise the task analysis of the skill. Providing help to a learner to perform a behavior as part of learning a new skill is accomplished through *prompting* by the teacher. The teacher provides help by giving one or more prompts to the learner for each step that the learner does not know how to perform.

There are several different types of prompts used in teaching programs with people who have developmental disabilities. The most common is a *verbal prompt*, in which help is provided through spoken (or manually signed) information. However, many people with developmental disabilities, and particularly those with more severe disabilities, have difficulty understanding spoken information such that other types of prompts are needed. A summary of the most common types of prompts used in teaching programs is provided in the following table.

Common Types of Prompts Used in Teaching Programs

Verbal – a spoken instruction or question that explains how, or directs how, to perform a step of a skill

Gestural – pointing, tapping, or any other body motion that provides information about what the learner should do to perform a step of a skill

Modeling – demonstrating or showing how to do part or all of a skill

Physical – manually guiding a learner through part (partial physical prompt) or all (full physical prompt) of a skill step

---

There are also other types of prompts used in teaching programs with some learners, such as pictures that show what to do, figures or drawings that show part or all of what to do, and written words for some learners. The selected readings on teaching procedures listed in the Table earlier in this chapter provide detailed information on these and other types of prompts. However, because the four types of prompts just illustrated -- verbal, gestural, modeling, physical -- are used most often in teaching programs with learners with developmental disabilities, these types of prompts are emphasized within the ***Teaching Skills Program***.

A key part of providing help to a learner to perform a new skill through prompting is the manner in which prompts are provided. How prompts are provided by the teacher pertains to both the type of prompt used and the specific way in which prompts are used. Most importantly, prompts should be provided consistently and systematically.

There are several main ways that prompts can be provided in a consistent and systematic manner. The ***Teaching Skills Program*** focuses on providing prompts in a *least-to-most helpful* manner. The least-to-most helpful prompting strategy has been shown repeatedly through applied research to represent an effective means of providing help through prompting. This approach also is one of the easiest prompting strategies for teachers to learn to apply consistently and systematically.

In the least-to-most helpful prompting process, the teacher provides help to a learner with a given skill step by initially providing the least amount of help that the learner appears to need to perform the step (e.g., a verbal prompt). If the learner does not perform the step with the help of the initial prompt, the teacher then provides a more helpful prompt for the same step, such as by partially guiding the learner's hand to perform the step (physical prompt). This process of providing successively more helpful prompts continues until the learner successfully completes the step, even if totally guiding the learner through the complete step is necessary (another type of physical prompt). The process of providing prompts in a least-to-most helpful fashion is illustrated below.

Illustration of a Least-To-Most Helpful Prompting Strategy

LEAST ── **MOST**

| verbal | gestural | modeling | partial physical guidance | full physical guidance |

The key feature of the least-to-most helpful prompting process is that successively more helpful or assistive prompts are provided until a learner completes the step being learned. Over time, the learner begins to complete the step with less and less help and eventually, without any help from the teacher. Again, this means of providing help is quite effective in most teaching programs.

The least-to-most helpful prompting process also allows considerable flexibility on the part of the teacher. Flexibility is built into the prompting strategy in that the teacher can determine what types of prompts to provide for each step of the skill being taught, as long as the prompts are provided in a least-to-most helpful manner. Some teachers may choose to follow a verbal prompt to perform a step with a partial physical prompt, whereas other teachers may follow the verbal prompt with a gestural prompt and then a partial physical prompt.

The prompting process just described is different than other types of teaching programs in which the teacher is directed to always use certain types of prompts. For example, some programs dictate that a teacher first use a verbal prompt, followed by a gestural prompt if the learner does not respond correctly to the verbal prompt, then followed by a partial physical prompt, and then by a full physical prompt if the learner still has not responded correctly. In contrast, in the approach emphasized here the teacher determines which types of prompts to use in each teaching situation. Which types of prompts are used in the least-to-most helpful fashion can be determined by the preferred style of the teacher, and what the teacher thinks is most beneficial for the learner.

Error Correction

When learners attempt to perform a step in a skill during a teaching program, one of three things can happen. First, the learner may not do anything due to not knowing what to do, or perhaps not wanting to do anything. When a learner does not respond to an instruction or other expectation to perform a step, the teacher responds with a more helpful prompt as described in the preceding section.

The second thing that can happen when a learner attempts to perform a step in a skill is that the learner performs the step correctly. When the learner correctly performs the designated step, the teacher should support the learner's performance by *reinforcing* the behavior. Reinforcement is discussed in the next chapter section. Finally, the third thing that can happen is the learner responds incorrectly by doing something other than the designated step in the skill – the learner makes an error. In the latter case, the teacher must correct the error.

It is critical that teachers correct any error a learner makes when attempting to perform a step in a skill that is being taught. When a learner incorrectly completes a step in the task analysis, learning how to perform the skill is hindered significantly. Additionally, every time a learner performs a step incorrectly, the learner is in essence learning to do the wrong thing. Performing a step incorrectly is particularly problematic for certain learners, such as many people with autism, because these individuals tend to prefer doing things in a set routine. Each time an error occurs, the learner is learning an incorrect routine or set of behaviors that becomes increasingly more difficult to correct.

When learners with developmental disabilities are being taught a new skill, errors will inevitably occur. Hence, teachers must be ready to correct the errors. In the ***Teaching Skills Program***, learner errors are corrected in the following manner:

- ***First*, the teacher instructs the learner to repeat the step in the task analysis at which the error occurred.**

- ***Second*, the teacher provides increased assistance through prompting to ensure the learner correctly completes the step on the second attempt.**

Using this error correction strategy, a teacher can minimize the number of errors made by a learner during the teaching session. The strategy also allows the teacher to quickly correct the error by immediately having the learner repeat the incorrectly completed step, and do so with enough teacher help to make sure the step is completed correctly on the second attempt. The following scenario illustrates the error correction strategy.

Illustration of an Error Correction Strategy When a Learner Performs a Step in the Task Analysis Incorrectly

A learner is being taught how to cook popcorn in a microwave. When the step to be completed involves pushing the picture for popcorn on the microwave to turn on the oven, the learner incorrectly pushes the picture of potatoes following the teacher's verbal prompt to push the picture button. The teacher then tells the learner that the wrong button was pushed and points to the picture of popcorn while simultaneously manually guiding the learner's finger to push the popcorn button.

In the illustration just provided, the error occurred when the learner pushed the wrong picture button on the microwave. The teacher then corrected the error by: (1) having the learner repeat the step where the error occurred (i.e., pushing a picture button on the microwave) and, (2) providing increased assistance by pointing to the picture and physically guiding the learner to push the correct picture button. In this manner, the error was quickly corrected through the teacher's actions.

Reinforcement

The final teaching component in the *Teaching Skills Program* is *reinforcement*. Reinforcement is a very powerful teaching strategy, and plays a critical role in both ensuring the effectiveness of teaching and making teaching enjoyable. As such, reinforcement will be described in detail in subsequent chapters that relate more specifically to ways to make teaching enjoyable for learners. This chapter section summarizes the role of reinforcement specifically for ensuring the effectiveness of teaching.

In its purest sense, reinforcement pertains to providing a desired consequence following an individual's behavior that increases the future occurrence of that behavior. That is, the individual will continue to engage in the behavior in order to obtain the desired consequence. Within teaching programs, reinforcement generally refers to the teacher providing consequences that support the learner in continuing to correctly perform steps in the task analysis that constitute the skill being taught.

There are two keys aspects of using reinforcement within the *Teaching Skills Program*. The most critical aspect is that the teacher should always provide a reinforcing consequence following the last step performed in the task analysis: *completion of the skill by the learner should always result in the learner receiving a reinforcing item or activity.* The second aspect pertains to the teacher providing reinforcing consequences periodically during the teaching session when the learner correctly completes various steps. The teacher can decide how often to follow correctly completed steps with a reinforcing consequence based on the teacher's view of how much support the learner needs to stay motivated. Again though, there should always be a reinforcing consequence following completion of the last step in the task analysis.

> **Reinforcement in the *Teaching Skills Program*:**
>
> Providing a reinforcing consequence following completion of the last step in the task analysis *and* providing a reinforcing consequence periodically during a teaching session following completion of various steps to help the learner be motivated to complete the steps.

An important decision when building reinforcement into teaching sessions is what will be used as the reinforcing consequence. This issue will be addressed later when discussing strategies for making teaching enjoyable for learners. However, generally the **Teaching Skills Program** focuses on teacher praise as the main reinforcer to support correct responding on the part of the learner. Praise for correctly completed steps by learners is usually quite effective as a means of motivating learner responding. Later chapters will discuss ways to enhance the degree to which teacher praise can motivate learning on the part of people with developmental disabilities.

Putting It All Together While Teaching

The discussion to this point regarding effective teaching has focused on the four main teaching components that should constitute a teaching program. As noted earlier though, effective teaching requires not only that a program be designed with evidence-based teaching strategies but also that the strategies be proficiently implemented by the teacher. Implementation refers to the manner in which the teacher uses the task analysis and carries out prompting, error correction, and reinforcement.

Proficient implementation of teaching programs can be enhanced if the teacher self-evaluates how well each teaching component is performed. The following checklist can be helpful for teachers to evaluate how well they implement each of the four basic teaching components.

Checklist for Evaluating Teaching Proficiency			
1. All steps taught in the proper order as listed on the task analysis?	Yes	No	NA
2. All prompts provided in a least-to-most helpful manner?	Yes	No	NA
3. All error corrections conducted such that each error is immediately corrected?	Yes	No	NA
4. Reinforcing consequence provided following the last step completed?	Yes	No	

The checklist is used to evaluate whether each of the four teaching components described in the preceding chapter sections was implemented appropriately during a teaching session. A "Yes" is scored if the respective component was correctly carried out or a "No" if the component was not carried out as discussed. In some cases, a "Yes" or "No" is not applicable (scored "NA" on the checklist). Specifically, in some cases there is only one step in the task analysis, such that order of teaching each step is not applicable. Also, if no more than a single prompt was necessary for each step, then a least-to-most helpful process would not be needed with additional prompts. Similarly, if no errors occurred by the learner such that no error correction was necessary by the teacher, then that respective component would be not applicable. More detailed information on using the checklist to evaluate teaching proficiency can be obtained by referring to **Appendix C**.

Qualification: Teaching New Skills Versus Requiring Compliance

As indicated in the preceding discussion, physical guidance is used as part of standard teaching procedures with people who have developmental disabilities. Physical guidance is often necessary as part of prompting strategies, and particularly with people who have more significant disabilities. Physical guidance is also a frequent part of error correction strategies. When physical guidance is used in these ways, it is important to note that the purpose is to teach learners skills that they do not know how to perform. The purpose is not to make individuals perform tasks involving skills that they already know how to do but do not want to perform.

Attempting to make people with developmental disabilities do something that they can do but do not want to perform represents attempts to evoke instruction following or compliance to requests. Instruction following and compliance are important skills for individuals with disabilities, as they are for people without disabilities. Nevertheless, it is important to recognize the difference between teaching new skills and attempting to obtain compliance.

Teaching new skills and obtaining compliance involve many of the same strategies on the part of support persons. For example, physical guidance can be used in both situations. However, the reasons for the strategies are different. When teaching a new skill to a learner, the learner typically needs help in performing steps comprising the skill because it is something that the learner does not know how to do independently. In contrast, when attempting to obtain compliance in doing something the learner already knows how to do, the learner needs help to be motivated to complete the requested task. Motivation can also be an issue when attempting to teach a new skill, but not to the degree involved in promoting compliance to complete a task that the learner simply does not want to do even though the learner has the necessary skills.

The distinction between using physical guidance to teach a new skill versus to obtain compliance is important for two reasons. First, the concern here is with helping individuals with disabilities learn new skills to function more independently and have more control over their lives. The intent is not to physically force a person to do something that is unwanted by the individual. Second, even though physical guidance in teaching is used to help an individual learn a new skill, the process can be unpleasant for the learner (see earlier discussion in **Chapter 1**). Special care is needed to provide physical guidance as part of the teaching process in a manner that the learner does not dislike. Ways to make teaching enjoyable and eliminate or significantly reduce any displeasure associated with physical guidance are discussed in-depth in the third section of this text.

When used in a teaching program, the purpose of physical guidance is to help a learner do something that the learner does not know how to do, not to force the learner to do something that the learner does not want to do.

Obtaining individual compliance with requests to do something that the learner knows how to do but does not want to perform is a different task on the part of the teacher relative to teaching a new skill. Our focus is on teaching new skills to learners in ways the learners find enjoyable. However, some of the same procedures to be discussed for making teaching enjoyable can be applied in situations in which the intent is to obtain compliance. In particular, if a teacher develops a good relationship with the learner, compliance to the teacher's requests to perform certain tasks can be enhanced significantly. **Chapter 5** elaborates on the importance of developing a good relationship with an individual with disabilities, and presents a detailed description of what can be done to establish such a relationship.

Chapter Review Questions

1. What are two common reasons why many teaching programs are not effective?

2. What are the four basic components of the **Teaching Skills Program**?

3. What are two advantages of using a task analysis in a teaching program?

4. What is meant by a least-to-most helpful prompt strategy (provide an example)?

5. Describe the error correction strategy in the **Teaching Skills Program** that should be used when a learner makes an error during teaching.

6. When should a reinforcing consequence always be given while carrying out a teaching program with a task analysis?

7. What is the distinction between teaching a new skill to a learner and attempting to obtain learner compliance in performing a skill that the learner has previously learned?

Chapter 4

Teaching for *Functional* Skill Development

The preceding chapter stressed the importance of ensuring teaching programs are *effective*. Teaching programs that are effective result in learners acquiring the skills that the programs are designed to teach. There is no reason to exert time and effort making programs enjoyable if the programs do not fulfill their main purpose of teaching new skills to learners with disabilities.

Equally important as the effectiveness of teaching is the nature of the skills being taught. Teaching programs should be designed to teach skills that are *functional*. Functional skills serve a meaningful purpose or function for the learner. The skills, once acquired by learners, help the learners function more independently or enjoyably in their day-to-day lives. Just as there is no reason to spend time making ineffective programs enjoyable, there is no reason to make teaching programs enjoyable if the programs are not designed to teach functional skills.

> **There is no justifiable reason to carry out teaching programs that do not result in learners acquiring skills or do not address skills that are functional for the learners.**

People who carry out teaching programs generally agree that the primary goal of the programs is for individual learners to acquire meaningful, functional skills. However, current practice in typical settings providing teaching services suggests that serious concern should be directed to the types of skills that programs are designed to teach.

Concern Regarding the Types of Skills Programs Are Designed to Teach

Concern over the types of skills targeted by teaching programs for learners with disabilities exists because many programs *do not* address meaningful or functional skills. Observations across the United States repeatedly have highlighted teaching programs that focus on skills that have no functional purpose for learners. Skills are taught in many settings, including school classrooms, adult activity centers, and sheltered workshops, that have no impact on increasing learner independence or enjoyment in their daily lives.

Understanding why teaching programs address nonfunctional skills can best be achieved by considering the theoretical foundation of educational services in the United States. The country's educational system is heavily based on a developmental model. According to the developmental model, people learn through a series of natural skill sequences that progress from simple to more complex skills. Before complex skills can be acquired, the simpler skills that form the earlier parts of the sequences must first be learned.

For people with disabilities who need help with the learning process, the developmental model dictates that skills should be taught in accordance with the natural sequence of learning simple skills before more complex skills. This approach to teaching has rather sound support for typically developing young children, and generally works well with that age group. However, for learners with developmental disabilities, the model breaks down from the perspective of teaching functional skills when learners are of an approximate middle school or junior high school age. The developmental model becomes even more problematic for adults with disabilities.

The problem with the developmental model for adolescents and adults who have developmental disabilities is several-fold. First, when the model is followed in its entirety, teaching programs for adolescents and adults often focus on skills that are normally taught to young children. Adults with disabilities, and especially people with severe disabilities, are frequently observed being taught to put pegs in pegboards, place rings on ring stacks, and string toy beads. While time is spent attempting to teach these pre-school types of skills, the individuals are receiving no teaching services directed to activities of daily living such as, for example, how to dress or groom, how to participate in leisure activities with their friends or neighbors, or how to prepare a snack for themselves. The latter skills can have a direct impact on adults with disabilities living more independently and enjoyably whereas the former skills have little effect on daily independence or enjoyment.

A second reason that the developmental model is problematic for people with disabilities beyond young children is that individuals do not learn skills exclusively in accordance with the typical developmental sequence. Individuals may not know how to perform a number of simple skills that occur early in the developmental sequence but be quite adept at performing more complex skills higher in the sequence. Listed below are common examples of individuals with developmental disabilities having learned relatively complex skills without having learned simpler skills that according to the developmental model, are necessary for learning the former skills.

- **An individual can independently purchase a soda from a vending machine even though the individual does not know the names of the specific coins used in the purchase**
- **An individual cannot read but knows the necessary dial settings on a microwave oven for cooking different foods**
- **An individual cannot tell time but knows when a favorite television show comes on**
- **An individual can independently dial a telephone to call a parent but cannot identify all the digits from 0 to 9 by name**

In these examples, individuals with disabilities have been taught skills that are more complex than what is considered developmentally to be simpler, pre-requisite skills. If teaching time was spent exclusively on teaching the pre-requisite skills that in and of themselves have no immediate utility for daily living, teachers would rarely have progressed to teaching the more functional skills.

To ensure teaching programs focus on skills that are truly functional for learners with disabilities, several useful guidelines have been developed. These guidelines, which have been well substantiated through applied research, differentiate functional from nonfunctional skills. Agencies and teaching personnel who have adopted the guidelines have demonstrated that learners with wide ranges of disabilities can learn functional skills using sound teaching practices. They have likewise demonstrated that there is no need for teaching programs that focus on nonfunctional skills.

In considering the guidelines to be presented in the remainder of this chapter, it is important to remember that the guidelines are intended for teaching programs involving adolescents and adults, not for young children. For the latter population, the developmental approach has important utility and generally should be adhered to when selecting skills to teach. Applications of the developmental model teach young learners skills that may not be immediately functional for daily living, but significantly enhance their subsequent learning of skills that are functional. Again though, the developmental model is much less helpful for teenage and adult learners. Teaching programs should focus on skills for teenagers and adults that are immediately useful and meaningful for these learners.

Guidelines for Determining Functional Skills For Teaching Programs Involving Teenagers and Adults

Guideline 1: Skills That Someone Typically Does For A Learner Are Functional Skills to Teach

This guideline is the oldest and most well established characteristic of a functional skill to teach to learners with disabilities. If a skill represents something that someone would typically do for a learner, then the skill would be functional to teach the learner to perform. The most common applications of this guideline pertain to teaching self-care skills. To illustrate, a support person would typically dress an individual if the individual did not have the skills to dress. Skills to dress independently would therefore represent functional skills to teach the individual. A support person likewise would brush an individual's hair if the person did not know how to use a hair brush. Learning how to use a hair brush would be a functional skill to teach.

In contrast to the types of skills just exemplified, teaching an individual how to dress a flannel board figure by placing small pieces of cloth on the figure would not meet this guideline for functional skills. If the learner does not know how to "dress" the figure, a support person would not routinely "dress" the figure for the individual. The intent of the program may be to help the individual learn dressing skills, but dressing a flannel board figure involves different skills than dressing oneself. It would be much more functional to directly teach the learner how to dress using the learner's own clothes.

There are many more examples of teaching programs designed to teach skills that do not directly involve the precise skills a learner needs to acquire. Generally these types of nonfunctional teaching programs can be avoided by following the guideline of *teaching skills that if a learner cannot perform, typically would be completed by someone for the learner.*

Guideline 2: The More Often A Skill Is Needed, The More Functional The Skill Is To Teach

This guideline pertains to a wide variety of skills. The guideline essentially involves determining how frequently various skills are likely to be used by a learner, and then teaching skills that are needed most often. Generally, the more frequently a learner needs to use a skill, the more functional the skill is for the learner.

The utility of this guideline is illustrated in a situation in which an individual moves into an apartment for the first time in a supported living arrangement. There are many domestic cleaning skills that would be helpful to teach the individual, but some skills are needed more often than others. For example, the skills to wash dishes would be needed much more frequently than the skills to wash windows. It would be more functional to teach the individual to wash dishes, as well as other daily cleaning skills, than to teach the individual to wash windows or similar skills needed only once a month. After the individual is taught the cleaning skills needed most frequently, programs can then be implemented to teach cleaning skills needed less frequently.

Another example of how this guideline can apply pertains to programs that focus on teaching a learner how to identify certain shapes. A number of teaching curricula include programs to teach learners to identify geometric shapes by name, such as squares, rectangles, and triangles. Being able to recognize and name different geometric shapes can be an important skill. However, this type of skill typically is not used very often. In contrast, identifying standard symbols such as male and female bathroom signs represents a skill that is likely to be used frequently. It would be more functional to teach the latter skill than the former.

> **It is generally more functional to teach skills needed frequently before teaching skills needed infrequently.**

Guideline 3: Skills That A Learner Would Be Paid To Complete As Part Of A Real Job Are Functional Skills To Teach

This guideline pertains to a more circumscribed set of skills than the first two guidelines. Specifically, the guideline involves skills exclusively in the vocational domain. The essence of the guideline is that if skills represent something that a learner could be paid to perform as part of a job, the skills are functional skills to teach.

This guideline is particularly relevant for helping adult learners obtain employment. Working in a paid job is not only necessary for allowing individuals with disabilities to earn an income, it is also a respected societal activity for adults. If individuals are to obtain employment, they must have skills to perform work tasks that comprise paid jobs.

This guideline is also especially important when considering the types of activities provided for adults with disabilities in congregate treatment settings such as adult activity centers, sheltered workshops, and adult education programs. Many adult day programs are still based on the developmental model summarized earlier. Due to reliance on the developmental approach, many day programs focus on work readiness skills in an attempt to prepare adults for eventual employment. Readiness programs address skills such as attending, instruction following, and staying seated at a table. Often the materials used in the activities are representative of materials typically provided for young persons. It is relatively common, for example, to see adults in day treatment programs spending time putting toy pegs in pegboards, sorting plastic chips, and putting child puzzles together.

Work readiness programs involving skills and materials such as those just exemplified have consistently been shown to have little value for adults with disabilities. Most notably, adults who are placed in these types of programs rarely graduate to placements in real jobs. The skills taught in work readiness programs also tend to have little relevance for those adults who eventually do obtain employment.

Research has repeatedly demonstrated that services intended to assist adults with disabilities in obtaining employment are more successful if they involve teaching programs that focus on skills constituting part or all of an actual job. Hence, instead of teaching an adult to put pegs in pegboards using the rationale of teaching attending-to-task skills, it is more functional to teach attending-to-task using an activity like putting ball point pens together. An individual is unlikely to ever obtain a job putting pegs in a pegboard whereas people do get paid to assemble pens in certain jobs.

> **Adults with disabilities can learn work readiness skills at the same time they are learning skills to actually perform job tasks.**

Using the guideline of teaching skills for which an individual could be paid to perform, the most functional vocational skills to teach are those that are in fact part of a real job. Adult day programs should strive to provide paid work for all participating adults with disabilities, even if the work is only part time. Learners can be taught the skills to complete the job while they are receiving pay for what they complete.

When paid jobs are not immediately available for respective consumers, then vocational programs should focus on teaching skills involved in jobs that are most likely to become available. The teaching programs should likewise involve real materials that would normally be used to complete the jobs instead of artificial or toy materials that often are used to simulate work materials.

Guideline 4: Leisure Skills Used By Age-Group Peers Without Disabilities Are Functional To Teach

This guideline addresses teaching what are considered to be *age appropriate* leisure skills to individuals with disabilities. Age appropriate leisure skills are those skills used during typical leisure activities by people without disabilities who are of the same age group as respective learners. Age groupings for determining age appropriateness usually include adulthood or beyond high school age, school age, and pre-school age.

There are many benefits of teaching people with disabilities leisure skills that are representative of the leisure pursuits of their same-age peers who do not have disabilities. In particular, when individuals with disabilities have skills to participate in leisure activities that their peers without disabilities engage in, then it is more likely individuals will take part in routine leisure activities with family members and friends. Participating in leisure activities with family members and friends is a common source of enjoyment for people, whether they have disabilities or not. In addition to the enjoyment factor, when individuals with disabilities participate in leisure activities with other people, they experience opportunities to learn and apply important social skills.

Another advantage of teaching leisure skills for participating in age appropriate activities pertains to how people with disabilities are treated by others. The following scenario illustrates the importance of age appropriate leisure skills in this regard.

CASE EXAMPLE

Mr. Garcia and Mr. Bennett have severe cognitive disabilities and reside together in a supported living arrangement. On Sunday afternoons a support staff usually accompanies Mr. Garcia and Mr. Bennett to the park in their home town. When at the park, Mr. Garcia typically plays with toy trucks in the sand box while Mr. Bennett likes to feed the ducks in the park pond. When people see Mr. Garcia in the sand box with his toy trucks, they usually avoid him and parents keep their children away from him. In contrast, people often feed the ducks at the pond and parents help their children feed the ducks in close proximity to Mr. Bennett. While jointly feeding the ducks, people occasionally interact with Mr. Bennett.

In this illustration, Mr. Garcia was doing something that is quite uncommon among adults during leisure time at the park; adults usually do not play with toy trucks in the sand. Consequently, Mr. Garcia was viewed by other visitors to the park as being strange and possibly threatening by some parents. People tended to avoid Mr. Garcia and parents would not let their children be in close proximity to him. In contrast, while feeding the ducks, Mr. Bennett was doing the same thing that other adult visitors did at the park. Mr. Bennett was engaging in a leisure activity that is quite normal for adults in that situation, and other adults felt comfortable being around him while participating in the same activity.

In short, individuals with disabilities are more likely to be treated in a friendly and respectful manner if they engage in leisure activities that are common for people to observe and perform. If individuals with disabilities frequently participate in leisure activities that are characteristic of individuals much younger than them, then they are likely to be stigmatized and avoided by their same-age peers.

> **Teaching people with disabilities age-appropriate leisure skills enhances their opportunities to interact with others and to be treated in a respectful manner.**

Although the benefits of individuals with disabilities participating in age appropriate activities in contrast to age inappropriate activities are well established, there is still some controversy when emphasizing age appropriate leisure skills. The controversy has some merit when considering the concept of leisure. By definition, leisure refers to times when a person can do what is desired (provided no one is harmed and no established rules or laws are broken). Correspondingly, a commonly held view is that people with disabilities should be allowed to do what they want during leisure time, even if the activities are not appropriate for their age group.

We support the notion that people with disabilities should not be strictly prohibited from engaging in desired leisure activities because the activities are not age appropriate, provided several criteria are met. The first criterion is that an individual should be given opportunities to engage in age appropriate leisure activities, even if the individual is likely to choose an alternative activity that is not age appropriate. In many cases, individuals engage in age inappropriate leisure activities because those are the only activities available. When no age appropriate leisure activities are available, then it is not clear that an individual truly desires the age inappropriate activity; the latter activity is the only thing that the individual can do at that time.

A second criterion for accepting the premise that an individual should be allowed to engage in an age inappropriate leisure activity if desired is that the individual should have the skills to participate in alternative, age appropriate activities. If the individual does not have the latter skills, then the person really does not have a choice to do something that is age appropriate. The individual engages in an age inappropriate activity essentially by default – that is the only activity for which the person has the skills to participate.

If people with disabilities are to acquire skills to participate in leisure activities that are characteristic of the leisure pursuits of their same-age peers, then teaching programs are needed to teach those skills. Individuals may not always choose to use age appropriate leisure skills they have been taught, but they will at least have a choice. If they have not been taught how to take part in leisure activities in which their peers participate, then there will be no choice but to engage in age inappropriate activities.

> **Although a case can be made for individuals to participate in leisure activities that are not appropriate for their age group under certain conditions, there is no reason to *intentionally teach* leisure skills that are not age appropriate.**

Guideline 5: Skills That Help An Individual Obtain Something Wanted Or Avoid Something Unwanted Without Problem Behavior Are Functional To Teach

This guideline is intended to provide teaching programs that help individuals with disabilities live their lives without problem behavior. There are numerous reasons why problem behavior such as aggression, property destruction, or self-injury occurs among people who have developmental disabilities. However, the vast majority of the reasons can usually be attributed to one of two factors. People with developmental disabilities engage in problem behavior to:

- **obtain something that is wanted**

- **avoid or escape something that is unwanted**

Using problem behavior to obtain something desired or to get out of something that is undesired occurs because individuals do not have the necessary skills to appropriately express their wants and discontents. Hence, a very functional set of skills to teach people with developmental disabilities is how to appropriately indicate what they do and do not want.

Selecting functional skills to teach learners as a means of avoiding problem behavior usually involves communication or social skills. For example, an individual may aggress toward a peer in an attempt to get a support person's attention. In this case the individual is using aggression to get something that is wanted. It would be functional to teach the individual how to approach and interact with the support person in a socially acceptable manner. Appropriately interacting with the support person would evoke the person's attention, thereby negating the need for the individual to aggress to obtain attention.

Using problem behavior to get out of something unwanted is not always as readily apparent to support persons as when an individual uses problem behavior to obtain attention or something else that is desired. However, using problem behavior in the former way is quite prevalent among many individuals with developmental disabilities who display problem behavior. A common illustration is when a support person requests an individual to do something that the individual does not want to do, such as cleaning a bedroom. The individual may strike at the support person in an attempt to get the person to leave the individual alone, and therefore not follow through with the request to clean the bedroom.

Problem behavior used by an individual to avoid or escape something unwanted can be prevented if the individual has the skills to express the displeasure in a socially acceptable manner. Hence, teaching the individual an appropriate means of indicating displeasure, whether through speaking, signing, or some other means of acceptable communication, can replace the need to engage in problem behavior.

Teaching appropriate ways to express desires and discontents is the most proactive means of helping individuals with developmental disabilities live their lives without problem behavior. Socially acceptable communication skills therefore represent very functional skills to teach. It should also be noted though that this means of preventing and eliminating problem behavior usually does not happen quickly. It takes time to teach communicative and social skills to an individual with a developmental disability. It also takes time to teach the individual appropriate situations in which to apply the newly learned skills.

As highlighted throughout this text, one situation that often occasions problem behavior among individuals with developmental disabilities is participation in formal teaching programs. Many learners will engage in problem behavior to avoid participating in a teaching session, or to get out of a session once initiated. A more immediate means of preventing problem behavior occasioned by a teaching program than teaching learners appropriate means of expressing their displeasure is to make the program enjoyable. If learners enjoy participating in a teaching program, then there is no reason to display problem behavior to avoid or escape the program.

> **Problem behavior displayed by a learner in an attempt to avoid or escape a teaching program can be prevented by making the program enjoyable for the learner.**

Subsequent chapters in this text describe in detail how to make teaching programs enjoyable for learners. The processes to be described make it highly unlikely that respective learners with disabilities will engage in problem behavior while participating in teaching sessions. However, individuals who display problem behavior during teaching programs are likely to show the same type of behavior in other, nonteaching situations. By teaching people appropriate ways to express their displeasure, problem behavior in the latter situations can also be prevented or eliminated.

Guideline 6: Skills That Are Highly Desired By Learners Are Functional To Teach

This guideline focuses on a basic purpose of teaching programs for learners with disabilities: to help them enjoy their lives. Skills that assist individuals to do things that they enjoy represent highly functional skills to teach. People with developmental disabilities cannot engage in activities they enjoy unless they have the skills required to participate in the activities.

Teaching skills that enable learners to do things they enjoy represents a person-centered approach to teaching. Person-centered means that supports and services provided for individuals with disabilities are designed around the most important desires of the individuals. Teaching functional skills that help individuals fulfill their personal desires is one critical component of person-centered supports and services.

It is beyond the scope of this text to thoroughly describe a person-centered approach. There are, however, a number of texts that discuss this means of determining personal desires of individuals with various types of disabilities, and helping individuals fulfill those desires (see **Person Centered Supports and Services** in the **Selected Readings**). The point of concern here is that one means of determining functional skills to teach a learner with a disability is to identify what the learner wants to learn.

SKILLS THAT ARE MEANINGFUL AND FUNCTIONAL TO TEACH LEARNERS WITH DEVELOPMENTAL DISABILITIES:

- Skills that would be completed by someone for a learner if the learner could not perform the skills

- Skills that a learner would use frequently

- Skills that a learner would be paid to perform as part of a job

- Skills used by same-age peers during leisure time

- Skills that help a learner get something wanted or get out of something unwanted without problem behavior

- Skills that are highly desired by a learner

Chapter Review Questions

1. *Briefly describe the developmental model in terms of skills selected to be taught to learners, and problems stemming from applications of the model for adult learners with developmental disabilities.*

2. *What are six guidelines for selecting functional skills to teach people who have developmental disabilities?*

3. *What is the oldest and most well-established guideline for selecting functional skills to teach?*

4. *What is the controversy regarding age-appropriate versus age-inappropriate leisure skills, and what are the two criteria that must be met for age-inappropriate leisure activities to be considered acceptable?*

5. *What does a person-centered approach to supports and services indicate regarding important skills to teach people with developmental disabilities?*

Section III
The Specifics for Making Teaching Enjoyable

Chapter 5
Developing A Good Teacher-Learner Relationship

Preceding chapters addressed two important pre-requisites for initiating efforts to make teaching programs enjoyable for learners with disabilities. First, programs should be designed in accordance with what evidence has shown to be effective teaching practices (**Chapter 3**). Second, programs should focus on skills that are functional and meaningful for individual learners (**Chapter 4**). This chapter addresses a third pre-requisite that is relevant for making teaching programs both effective and enjoyable: developing a good relationship between the teacher and learner.

**Pre-Requisites for Making Teaching
Effective and Enjoyable**

Availability and implementation of evidence-based teaching procedures

Targeting functional and meaningful skills for teaching

Development of a good teacher-learner relationship

Having a good relationship with a learner is critical for a teacher to make teaching enjoyable for individuals with developmental disabilities. A good relationship enhances the effectiveness of every other procedure to be described for making teaching programs enjoyable. Although the procedures to be discussed in subsequent chapters can increase learner enjoyment with a teaching program even if there is not a particularly good relationship between the teacher and learner, the procedures will be much more successful if a good relationship does exist.

The importance of a good relationship between teachers and learners is well accepted. There is widespread recognition that the best teachers are those who are not only skilled in the technology of teaching, but also have the ability to establish a good relationship with their learners.

Although there is a strong consensus regarding the importance of teachers having a good relationship with their learners, what exactly constitutes a good relationship is not so clearly recognized. Confusion over the specifics of a good relationship presents serious problems when attempting to make teaching programs enjoyable for learners. Without clear identification of what constitutes a good relationship, it is difficult if not impossible for teachers to know what to strive to attain. Lack of specification also impedes knowing what can be done to achieve the desired rapport with a learner.

For purposes of enhancing teaching effectiveness, as well as for making teaching enjoyable for a learner, the essence of a good relationship is that the *learner enjoys interacting with the teacher.* When a teacher has a good relationship with a learner, the learner likes it when the teacher talks to or otherwise interacts with the learner. The learner also will seek out the teacher's attention, and will work to please the teacher to receive the teacher's praise.

The essence of good teacher-learner relationship is that the learner enjoys interacting with the teacher.

Considering a good relationship from a teaching perspective as a learner enjoying interactions with the teacher has strong logical appeal. All of us, whether we have disabilities or not, enjoy interacting with some people more than others. We also tend not to enjoy interacting with some persons at all. Because carrying out teaching programs involves rather intense and frequent interactions between teachers and learners, it is logical that learners would enjoy teaching sessions more if the sessions involve someone with whom they like to interact.

A good relationship between a teacher and learner does not occur automatically or immediately. Rather, certain events must take place over time for the relationship to develop. Before describing what should occur to develop a good teacher-learner relationship, difficulties encountered when a good relationship has not been developed warrant mention. Such difficulties highlight the importance of taking specific actions to develop a good relationship to make teaching enjoyable for learners with developmental disabilities.

Difficulties Encountered When A Good Teacher-Learner Relationship Does Not Exist

Most of the difficulties encountered when a good relationship has not been developed between a teacher and learner stem from those features of teaching strategies that tend to be inherently disliked by learners. As indicated in **Chapter 1**, teaching people with developmental disabilities involves repeated teacher instructions presented to the learner. Repeated instructions are often unpleasant – most people do not like to be told repeatedly to do something. People particularly do not like to be told to do something by persons with whom they do not like to interact. Hence, the lack of a good relationship between a learner and teacher makes instructions much more disliked relative to situations in which the learner enjoys interacting with the teacher.

Teaching sessions with people who have developmental disabilities also require close physical proximity between the teacher and learner. Close physical proximity is necessary to appropriately carry out various teaching strategies, such as prompting and correcting errors. Learners with disabilities, as with people without disabilities, like it when certain individuals are physically close to them but not when other individuals are in close proximity. People generally prefer to have someone in close physical proximity whom they like to interact with, and not individuals with whom they do not like to interact. Consequently, when a teacher who does not have a good relationship with a learner moves within close physical proximity to carry out a teaching program, the learner can experience serious displeasure.

Learner dislike with a teacher being in close physical proximity (when there is not a good relationship between the learner and teacher) is intensified when the proximity involves physical contact between the teacher and learner. As with close proximity, physical contact between a teacher and learner is often a necessary part of teaching procedures. Learners enjoy or do not mind being touched by some people, but seriously dislike being touched by other individuals. Generally, the latter persons are people with whom learners do not like to interact.

In short, the potentially inherent unpleasantness of certain teaching practices that constitute effective teaching programs becomes magnified when teaching is conducted by someone with whom the learner does not like to interact. Taking the time to develop a good relationship with a learner prior to beginning a teaching program prevents magnification of such unpleasantness. In many cases, the development of a good relationship can actually turn those unpleasant features into actions that learners begin to enjoy.

Why A Good Teacher-Learner Relationship Is Not Always Developed

Despite recognition of the importance of establishing a good relationship and the difficulties arising when such a relationship is not developed, many teaching programs are conducted without a good teacher-learner relationship. There are several reasons why teaching programs are carried out without a teacher first establishing rapport with a respective learner, but three reasons are most prevalent:

- **The teacher does not take the time to develop a good relationship**

- **The teacher does not know exactly what to do to develop a good relationship**

- **The teacher is unfamiliar with the learner**

In most cases when teaching programs are carried out even though a good teacher-learner relationship has not been developed, the teacher has not spent the necessary time to develop rapport with the learner. Teachers may be aware of the need to develop rapport prior to teaching, but are unable to find sufficient time to spend with the learner to establish a good relationship. The latter situation is common in settings in which staff charged with teaching responsibilities work with many individuals with disabilities, such as special education classrooms, group homes, and adult activity centers.

A second reason teachers do not develop a good relationship with a learner is because teachers are not sure exactly what they should do to develop such a relationship. Most support personnel are not specifically trained in procedures for establishing rapport with people with developmental disabilities. As such, even if teachers are aware of the importance of establishing rapport with individuals whom they are expected to teach, they do not know how to develop a good relationship.

The third major reason that teaching programs are carried out even though a good relationship has not been developed is that the responsible teacher is unfamiliar with the learner; the teacher has not been able to establish a relationship because the teacher has not interacted with the learner very much. This situation exists frequently in residential settings in which different shifts of direct support staff work with residents of the homes. Often some staff work primarily with certain residents while other staff work with other residents. When the former staff are not present at work, the latter staff must implement the teaching programs that the former staff usually carry out – even though the staff are not very familiar with the residents.

A similar, and more problematic, situation occurs in residential settings when staff absences occur and staff from another residence are temporarily re-assigned or "pulled" to work in the residence to cover for the absent staff. The re-assigned staff are then expected to carry out teaching programs for residents in the homes to which they are re-assigned, despite having very little if any familiarity with the residents whom they will be teaching. A related situation occurs in school classrooms with substitute teachers, or when teacher assistants are "pulled" from one class to another.

When teachers are expected to carry out teaching programs with learners with whom they have little familiarity, all the problems noted earlier with teaching without a good relationship are seriously compounded. In such situations, not only has there been no opportunity to develop a good teacher-learner relationship, the teacher also does not know the personal preferences of the learner. Additionally, the teacher is not familiar with the learner's idiosyncratic means of communicating likes and dislikes. Essentially every individual with significant developmental disabilities has idiosyncratic ways of communicating, and the only true means to learn those ways is to have repeated interactions with the learner.

When a teacher attempts to teach a learner without being able to understand the learner's communication attempts, the teaching process usually becomes frustrating for the learner and most unpleasant. Often, learners will resort to problem behavior in attempts to communicate with the teacher, such as engaging in aggression to avoid doing something the learner does not understand or does not want to perform. The end result is the teaching process is clearly not an enjoyable activity for the learner. This type of situation should be avoided as much as possible. It rarely results in effective teaching and almost always is unpleasant for the learner.

> **Teachers should not attempt to carry out teaching programs, nor be expected to carry out programs, with learners whom the teachers do not know very well.**

How To Develop A Good Teacher-Learner Relationship

Familiarity between a teacher and learner is critical for making teaching enjoyable for individuals with developmental disabilities. However, familiarity alone is not sufficient. Being familiar with a potential learner does not ensure that the teacher will have a good relationship with the learner, only that the teacher and learner have become acquainted with each other. Familiarity between teacher and learner will enhance learner enjoyment with a teaching program only if the familiarity is accompanied by the learner developing a desire to interact with the teacher.

> **Familiarity between teacher and learner is necessary for developing a good teacher-learner relationship but not sufficient; the learner must also develop a desire to interact with the teacher.**

While a teacher is becoming familiar with a learner and vice versa, specific events must occur for the learner to begin to like interacting with the teacher. Again, a learner enjoying interactions with a teacher is the basis of a good teacher-learner relationship.

Before discussing what can be done to promote learner enjoyment in interacting with a teacher, a common myth regarding teacher-learner relationships should be noted. It is often assumed that a teacher-learner relationship is something that develops naturally, based in large part on the personality of the teacher. It is further assumed that some teachers inherently have the right personality to develop good relationships with learners and some do not.

It is clear that some support persons who have teaching responsibilities tend to have better relationships with respective learners than other support persons. A common illustration is with individuals who have frequent problem behavior. When certain staff are present in the individuals' environment, the individuals rarely display the problem behavior. A similar occurrence in many settings is that an individual will respond better to instructional requests of certain staff members than to requests of other staff.

In the illustrations just provided, the staff who occasion less problem behavior, or enhance instruction following by a given individual, have established a good relationship with the individual. The learner enjoys interacting with the staff, and generally feels more comfortable with them relative to other staff. This does not mean however, that the differences in relationships between various staff and the respective individual are due to personality differences among the staff. Rather, the differences are due to how the staff have interacted with the individual in the past.

Good teacher-learner relationships are not an all-or-none phenomenon, and staff do not simply have the right or wrong personality necessary to develop a good relationship. Contrary views, though popular in many settings, represent a serious misconception or myth. If staff interact in desirable ways with individuals with developmental disabilities, most if not all staff can develop a good teacher-learner relationship. There are three basic things staff can do to establish such a relationship:

- **Spend time helping the learner do things the learner enjoys**

- **Help the learner avoid or escape things the learner does not like to do**

- **Learn to communicate well with the learner**

Spend Time Helping The Learner Do Things The Learner Enjoys

The best way for a teacher to help a learner enjoy interactions is for the teacher to spend time doing things with the learner that the learner enjoys. Before a teaching program is initiated with a learner, the teacher should have specific times set aside each day for the sole purpose of helping the learner have fun. In this manner, the learner not only becomes more familiar with the teacher and vice versa, the learner begins to enjoy being with the teacher.

Spending selected periods of time doing things with a learner with the goal of helping the learner have fun is most important when a teacher plans to begin a teaching program with a new learner (i.e., a learner with whom the teacher has not interacted with in the past or otherwise does not know very well). For example, if a special education teacher has a new student assigned to the classroom, the teacher should spend some time each day doing things with the student that the student enjoys before initiating teaching programs with the student. After a week or so of engaging in enjoyable activities with the learner each day, it will usually be apparent that the learner is beginning to enjoy interacting with the teacher.

Another situation in which it is critical for a teacher to spend specific periods of time doing things with the sole purpose of helping a learner have fun is when a teacher has observed resistance on the part of the learner to previous teaching attempts. If it becomes apparent that teaching sessions are unpleasant for a learner, the teacher should temporarily discontinue the sessions. The teacher should then work on improving the relationship with the learner by spending one-on-one time doing things the learner enjoys. Once the teacher observes that the learner is enjoying the latter activities, the teacher can then re-initiate the teaching sessions. In these situations it is also most helpful to incorporate other strategies within the teaching process as discussed in subsequent chapters to enhance the learner's enjoyment.

Most Important Situations for a Teacher to Spend Specific Periods of Time Helping a Learner Have Fun:

When the teacher is going to be carrying out a teaching program with a new learner.

When a learner has shown resistance to previous teaching programs.

Generally, if a teacher spends some time each day doing things with a learner for the sole purpose of learner enjoyment, it only takes about one week for the learner to begin to enjoy interacting with the teacher. However, even after a teaching program is initiated with a learner, it is advantageous for the teacher to continue having certain times during the day devoted to doing things with a learner that the learner enjoys. Every classroom, group home, workshop, and any other setting in which formal teaching programs are conducted with people who have developmental disabilities should have time set aside every day for teachers to involve learners in enjoyable activities.

Conducting enjoyable activities involving a teacher and learner helps to maintain and further develop the teacher-learner relationship. These activities should occur in addition to formal teaching sessions that are conducted, although the goal is to make the teaching sessions enjoyable as well. Conducting daily activities that a learner enjoys, or at least as close to daily as realistically possible, also helps the learner associate the overall environment in which the teaching occurs with general enjoyment.

> **Teachers should strive to conduct enjoyable activities every day with each learner for whom the teacher carries out teaching programs.**

In order for a teacher to spend time with a learner to help the learner enjoy interacting with the teacher, the teacher must be knowledgeable about specific activities in which the learner likes to participate. Teachers who already have familiarity with a learner usually have a good idea about favorite activities of the learner. In cases where a teacher is not sure about favorite learner activities despite familiarity with the learner, or if the learner is new to the teacher, specific actions must be taken to find out what the learner enjoys. In general, such actions typically involve one or more of the following:

- **Ask the learner and/or people who know the learner well what the learner's most favorite activities involve**

- **Observe what the learner does during free time**

- **Give the learner discrete choices of things to do and observe what activities the learner chooses**

Each of the ways of identifying what a person with a developmental disability enjoys as just listed will be described in-depth in subsequent chapters (see in particular **Chapter 8**). The point of concern here is that enjoyable activities involving the teacher and learner, however identified, should occur frequently to help establish a good teacher-learner relationship.

Help The Learner Avoid or Escape Things That Are Disliked

Another way to help develop a good teacher-learner relationship is for the teacher to assist the learner in avoiding or escaping things that the learner does not like. Helping a learner *avoid* things that the learner does not like involves the teacher preventing things from happening that tend to displease or bother the learner. Assisting a learner to *escape* things that the learner does not like involves a teacher changing or stopping an action when the teacher observes that the learner does not like the ongoing event.

When a teacher helps a learner avoid or escape undesired events and activities, the learner begins to associate the teacher with reducing unpleasantness in the learner's environment. This association has a similar effect as that noted earlier of the learner associating the teaching setting (and the teacher) with enjoyable events and activities; the learner begins to associate the teacher with making the learner's environment less unpleasant and therefore, more desirable. Teachers should be very vigilant regarding certain things that learners tend not to like within a respective teaching setting and change or remove those things whenever possible.

> **Teachers can make a teaching setting more enjoyable for a learner, and enhance their relationship with the learner, by conducting activities the learner likes and changing or removing activities the learner does not like.**

In most teaching settings there are likely to be certain activities a learner may not enjoy that can not or should not be removed from the teaching setting. Nonetheless, essentially every environment also has some things a respective learner does not like that a teacher could help the learner avoid or escape. For example, a learner may become upset whenever another student or client is nearby. When a teacher observes another person is approaching the learner whom the learner does not appear to like, the teacher can direct the person elsewhere or help the learner move someplace else. Similarly, a teacher may observe that a learner becomes upset when there is a staff shift change in a group home or when a particular environment becomes especially noisy or active. In such cases the teacher could help the learner escape the situation by escorting the learner to another location or involve the learner in an enjoyable activity that re-directs the learner's attention away from the ongoing situation.

The best way for teachers to be aware of what events and activities a learner tends to dislike is to carefully observe the learner's reactions when different events and activities occur. When a teacher begins interacting with a new learner, it is also wise for the teacher to talk with other people who know the learner and ask them what specific things the learner tends to dislike.

> **Teachers should carefully observe learner reactions to different events and activities to determine what the learner does not like.**

Learn To Communicate With A Learner

The importance of a teacher being able to communicate effectively with a learner was noted previously. However, for basically the same reasons that teachers do not always develop good relationships with learners, many teachers do not learn to communicate well with respective learners. When teachers do not know how to communicate effectively with learners, carrying out teaching programs always becomes problematic, and rarely represents an enjoyable experience for learners.

Learning to communicate well with a learner who has a developmental disability means that the teacher can understand and respond to the learner's existing method of communicating. Of course in many cases, the goal of a teaching program may be to help a learner acquire a conventional means of communicating. Even with the latter teaching programs though, the teacher must be able to understand and respond to the learner's existing communication attempts while the learner is being taught a more effective means of communicating.

> **Teachers must be able to understand and respond to a learner's existing means of communicating.**

Many people with developmental disabilities have limitations with use of conventional speech for communication purposes. Consequently, many learners have other means of communicating in addition to, or instead of, normal speech. Teachers must be able to understand and respond to those means of communication. If the learner uses sign language, the teacher must be able to use the same type of sign language. If the learner uses a voice output communication device or other type of augmentative communication device, the teacher must use that device for interacting with the learner. Most importantly, teachers must learn to understand and respond to idiosyncratic vocalizations and mannerisms the learner uses to communicate.

Effective communication between a teacher and learner cannot be taken for granted. Some learners know more manual signs, for example, than their teachers such that teachers are limited in the degree to which effective communication can occur. For learners who use augmentative communication devices, teachers may not know how to keep the devices operable. In other cases, there may be problems in ensuring that a communication device remains with a learner from one setting to another (e.g., from the learner's residence to day treatment site or vice versa). Most commonly though, teachers simply have not learned all of a learner's idiosyncratic sounds and mannerisms that the learner relies on for communication purposes.

In order for teachers to learn how to communicate with the learners whom they will teach, teachers must spend time interacting with the learners prior to implementing a teaching program. Learning how to communicate with a learner is one beneficial outcome of spending time conducting enjoyable activities for a learner as described earlier. While the teacher is interacting with the learner during a desired activity, the teacher will usually acquire important information about how to effectively communicate with the learner.

For teachers who are about to begin teaching programs with learners with whom they are not very familiar, it is most helpful if the teachers talk with people who know the learner in order to find out how the learner typically expresses likes and dislikes. It can also be helpful if teachers spend time observing people familiar with the learner interact with the learner to directly see how the learner communicates. Until a teacher is confident in how to understand and respond to the learner's existing communication means, the teacher should not begin a formal teaching program with the learner.

> **A teacher should never initiate a teaching program until the teacher can readily understand a learner's existing means of communicating.**

Overcoming Common Obstacles to Establishing a Good Teacher-Learner Relationship

Working to develop a good relationship with a learner usually constitutes an enjoyable process for both the learner and teacher. Spending time doing things that the learner enjoys, helping the learner avoid and escape unpleasant events, and getting to know the learner's communication style typically represent pleasant experiences. However, there are also some common obstacles to performing these activities that interfere with the overall development of a good teacher-learner relationship. These include:

- **Lack of sufficient time to work on relationship building**

- **Supervisory interference or lack of support for spending time doing things necessary to develop a good relationship**

- **Apprehension, or even fear, on the part of the teacher to work with some learners**

Lack of Time to Work on Relationship Building

Performing the activities necessary to develop a good teacher-learner relationship takes time. Such activities usually must occur for at least a week, and often longer for learners who have highly serious communication difficulties, before initiating a teaching program.

Teachers may experience difficulty scheduling specific times during the day to conduct the types of relationship-building activities discussed to this point. Nonetheless, from the perspective of making subsequent teaching programs enjoyable for learners, the time is well spent. Time spent building a good relationship also can reduce the time necessary to successfully complete teaching responsibilities because learners respond better and learn more quickly when they enjoy interacting with a teacher.

In most settings in which formal teaching programs are carried out with individuals who have developmental disabilities, sufficient time to schedule specific relationship-building activities generally exists. The activities discussed in preceding chapter sections can usually be accomplished in less than 20 minutes at a time with a given learner. A problem may still arise though in determining what other activities may have to be omitted or postponed from the day's usual schedule. Conducting specific relationship-building activities should be given a priority relative to other activities. In many cases, if relationship-building activities are not given adequate priority to conduct, future attempts to carry out teaching programs are likely to be futile.

Supervisor Interference or Lack of Support

Often a more difficult obstacle to building a relationship than apparent lack of time is supervisor interference or lack of support for spending time on activities for the primary purpose of relationship building. Some supervisors may question why time is being spent, for example, simply doing things to help a learner enjoy being with the teacher relative to time spent with more traditional work responsibilities. Other supervisors may actively criticize teachers who spend time on various relationship-building activities in lieu of carrying out formal teaching programs. Such supervisory actions can make the job of the teacher difficult and unpleasant.

Specific roles of supervisors in making teaching enjoyable for people with developmental disabilities will be discussed in **Chapter 11**. Suffice it to say at this point that teachers should explain the rationale for their actions to supervisors. Explanations regarding why it is necessary to spend time helping a learner enjoy interactions with the teacher and other relationship-building activities should be provided to supervisors before such activities are initiated. In this manner, if a supervisor happens to observe the activities, the supervisor will have some knowledge as to their purpose. Typically when supervisors know the purpose of various activities prior to observing them, the supervisors are more understanding and accepting relative to situations in which supervisors unexpectedly observe the activities without any pre-understanding of their purpose.

Teacher Apprehension of Working With Certain Learners

Though not always readily acknowledged, human service personnel sometimes are apprehensive about working with certain individuals who have developmental disabilities. In the worst-case scenarios, staff experience significant fear about working with some individuals. Apprehension and fear are most common among new staff in support settings, but can also occur among highly experienced personnel. Feelings of apprehension or fear seriously impede a teacher's ability to spend time with a learner to develop a good relationship, and must be alleviated.

> **Teachers cannot be expected to spend time developing a relationship with a learner if the teachers experience apprehension or fear about working with the learner.**

Feelings of apprehension or fear are especially likely to occur when a teacher is expected to work with a learner who has shown resistance to previous teaching programs. A number of individuals with developmental disabilities who demonstrate resistance to teaching display one or more seriously challenging behaviors. Such behaviors, including aggression, self-injury, and property destruction, can cause harm to others or themselves. A teacher cannot be expected to spend time developing enjoyable interactions with a learner if the teacher is afraid of being hurt, or others being harmed, by the learner.

Feelings of apprehension or fear on the part of a teacher must be acknowledged by the teacher. Such feelings must also be brought to the attention of the teacher's supervisor. In turn, the supervisor must acknowledge the apprehension or fear, and take active steps to remedy the situation. Specific steps the supervisor can take are discussed in **Chapter 11**. The point of concern here is that effective and enjoyable teaching cannot occur when the teacher is apprehensive or fearful about interacting with a given learner. The teacher must be provided with assistance to rectify the situation and overcome the apprehension or fear.

Chapter Review Questions

1. *What are three pre-requisites for making teaching effective and enjoyable?*

2. *What is the essence of a good teacher-learner relationship (i.e., what must become apparent to demonstrate that such a relationship exists)?*

3. *What are three common reasons why a good teacher-learner relationship is not developed?*

4. *What are three things a teacher should do to develop a good relationship with a learner before initiating a teaching program?*

5. *Why are some supervisors likely to interfere with certain actions teachers take to establish good relationships with learners, and what can teachers do to reduce the likelihood of such interference?*

6. *What is the effect of teacher apprehension about working with a learner on learner enjoyment with a teaching program, and what should a teacher do about the apprehension?*

Chapter 6

Organizing A Teaching Session For Learner Enjoyment: The *Preferred Antecedent, Behavior, Consequence* Model

Once the pre-requisites for making teaching enjoyable have been met as described in preceding chapters, the next step is to organize a teaching session to make it enjoyable for the learner. As subsequent chapters will describe, there are many specific procedures to incorporate within a teaching session to enhance learner enjoyment. To obtain maximum benefit from the various procedures, it is helpful if an organizational framework is used to initially plan and then conduct the session. That framework is represented in the *Antecedent, Behavior, Consequence (ABC) Model of Preference-Based Teaching*.

The *ABC Model of Preference-Based Teaching*, or *Preferred ABC Model*, pertains to what should be done: (1) immediately prior to beginning a teaching session (antecedent), (2) in association with teacher and learner behavior during and between instructional trials (behavior) and, (3) immediately after the teaching session is completed (consequence). The essence is to ensure that activities or events a learner enjoys are built into each of these three parts of the teaching process. Each part warrants attention before a teaching program is initiated to ensure the teaching process will be enjoyable for the learner.

A general approach to making teaching sessions enjoyable is to conduct activities the learner prefers *before*, *during*, and *after* each session.

Conducting Enjoyable Antecedent Activities

A key step for making a teaching session enjoyable for a learner is to set the occasion for teaching in a way the learner enjoys. Activities the learner prefers and enjoys should be conducted as antecedent events to a teaching session. The intent is to increase the learner's level of enjoyment when the teaching session is just about to begin.

In one sense, the purpose of conducting preferred antecedent events is to help the learner be in a "good mood" when actual teaching is initiated. Being in a "good mood" means that a learner is enjoying the immediate situation, or what is ongoing in the surrounding environment. When a learner enjoys what is going on in the surrounding environment, that enjoyment can carry over to subsequent teacher actions involved in presenting instructional trials. Additionally, when a learner is enjoying the immediate situation, the learner frequently becomes more responsive to teacher requests and instructions, which in turn facilitates the teaching process. A type of momentum of learner enjoyment and responsiveness is established that continues into the teaching process.

The benefits of promoting learner enjoyment before beginning a teaching session can be appreciated by considering what often happens when a learner is not enjoying the immediate situation, or is in a "bad mood" when it is time to begin a teaching program. Most support personnel who have carried out teaching programs have likely experienced the negative reactions of individuals who, for whatever reason, are clearly unhappy when it is time to conduct a teaching program. Signs of unhappiness, or being in a "bad mood", are frequently followed by resistance to teaching that ranges from repeated complaints to serious aggression toward the teacher in attempts to avoid participating in the program. Although not always officially sanctioned within teaching settings, many experienced support personnel have learned that it is best to forego a teaching program when a particular learner is in a "bad mood" or is otherwise having a "bad day".

There are two general approaches for using antecedent activities to enhance learner enjoyment and responsiveness prior to beginning a teaching session. The first approach involves arranging the physical environment to the learner's liking. The second involves the teacher interacting with the learner in ways the learner enjoys.

Arranging the Teaching Environment to the Learner's Liking

Arranging the environment to the learner's liking involves two steps. The first step is to alter the environment to include various physical attributes that the learner appears to prefer or like. The second step is to remove aspects of the physical environment that the learner appears to dislike or not prefer.

Arranging an environment to include features a learner likes and exclude features a learner dislikes requires a teacher to have a good knowledge of a learner's individual preferences. This is one reason why it is critical for a teacher to spend time getting to know a learner and establishing rapport with the learner as discussed in the preceding chapter; the process usually results in the teacher identifying respective preferences of the learner. **Chapters 7** and **8** describe additional procedures for identifying environmental preferences of individuals with varying degrees of developmental disabilities.

> **Prior to beginning a teaching session, the teacher should alter the physical environment to add features the learner likes and remove features the learner does not like.**

On one extreme, changing an environment to make it more desirable for a learner involves escorting the learner to a separate or discrete physical location (i.e., essentially changing the entire environment) before implementing a teaching program. For example, some individuals prefer to work in quiet places separate from other learners. Hence, it can be advantageous to arrange a special, quiet room if possible that is used just for carrying out individual teaching programs. Other individuals simply like having a special place that is reserved only for them and their teacher. In the latter case, respective individuals may look forward to times when the teacher arranges teaching sessions to occur in their "special" location. The following case example illustrates how a special place that is preferred by a learner can be used to increase the learner's enjoyment with the teaching process.

CASE EXAMPLE

Eleanor, an older adult who was learning a supported job in a publishing company, often expressed displeasure when being instructed on a work task. Eleanor expressed her displeasure by grunting and other negative sounds, and periodically refusing to work. When given an opportunity to work in a company supervisor's office with just her job coach instead of her usual work area in a large work room with other supported workers, Eleanor almost always chose to work in the office. When in the office she tended to respond to instructions in a more pleasant manner by smiling and laughing. Eleanor also complied more readily with her job coach's instructions in the office and rarely refused to do her work.

In a number of teaching settings, it may not be possible to change the entire environment by moving to another room for teaching purposes, or a respective learner may not want to leave the immediate area. In these cases there may be a part of the existing area that is preferred by a learner that can be used for teaching purposes.

CASE EXAMPLE

Jonathon worked in the same publishing company as Eleanor and was also being taught a new job skill. Jonathon likewise indicated periodic displeasure with work-related teaching instructions as indicated by repeatedly stomping his feet and refusing to work. When given an opportunity to perform his work in front of a window in the work room, he greatly reduced his foot stomping and work refusal. Working in front of the window was tried with

Jonathon after one of his support staff indicated that he really enjoyed looking at trucks and cars. By moving his work area to the window, Jonathon was able to occasionally watch vehicles passing by on the road outside of the window while receiving instruction on the new job skill.

Besides changing where a teaching session is conducted, an environment may be made more preferred for a learner by altering certain physical aspects of the environment to suit the learner's liking. To illustrate, some individuals enjoy having a favorite personal possession present during a teaching session such as a cap or purse. It should be noted though that any changes to make the environment more attractive to an individual should be made with consideration of the individual's ability to attend to subsequent teaching procedures. Environmental changes that seriously reduce a person's ability to attend to the teacher should not be made.

Environments in which a teaching session will occur can also be made more desirable for learners by removing certain features the individuals tend to dislike. For example, waiting until other persons, such as other students in a classroom, are temporarily out of the immediate environment before conducting a teaching session may make the teaching situation more preferred and less distracting for a learner. Other learners prefer situations in which one particular peer is not around, such that conducting a teaching session when the latter individual is not present can represent a means of enhancing the desirability of an environment for the learner.

In considering ways to make environments more desirable for individuals with developmental disabilities to help set the occasion for an enjoyable teaching session, the importance of knowing individual learner preferences warrants repeating. Whereas some learners prefer minimal environmental stimulation, others prefer environments with a considerable amount of ongoing activity or stimulation. People with developmental disabilities, like everybody else, have individual preferences. Those preferences must be determined prior to planning how to conduct teaching sessions if the teaching is going to be truly enjoyable for the learner.

> **Making an environment in which a teaching session will occur desirable for a learner requires that the teacher clearly identify specific preferences of the learner.**

Interacting With a Learner to Enhance Enjoyment

In addition to changing the physical environment prior to conducting a teaching session, antecedent activities for making teaching enjoyable involve the teacher interacting with the learner in ways the learner enjoys. Typically, such interactions involve conducting a brief activity or two that the learner likes. Some of the antecedent activities we and our colleagues have used as part of procedures for enhancing learner enjoyment with an immediately forthcoming teaching program include:

- Briefly massaging a learner's shoulders
- Joking with a learner for a few minutes
- Softly talking to a learner in a quiet location
- Swinging in a hammock for a few minutes
  (in this case the subsequent teaching trials occurred in the hammock)
- Letting the learner play with some of the materials that will be used in the teaching trials for a few minutes

As the activities just noted illustrate, what is done by the teacher immediately before beginning a formal teaching session must be highly individualized. This requirement again underscores the importance of identifying individual learner preferences in order to set the occasion for an enjoyable teaching experience – in this case, learner preferences for specific activities.

Another consideration when selecting antecedent activities to precede a teaching session pertains to keeping the activities brief – usually no more than three to five minutes. What is done immediately before a teaching session should be viewed essentially as the beginning of the overall teaching process. Environmental changes and teacher activities prior to initiating teaching trials should not be structured to represent a discrete set of events that appear separate from the teaching trials. Once the antecedent events are begun, it should be clear to the learner that these events will lead directly into the formal teaching session.

It is important that antecedent events lead directly into the beginning of teaching trials without any apparent break to avoid the learner becoming overly involved in the antecedent activities. If the learner begins to view the antecedent events as a discrete set of activities, then the learner can become reluctant to have the activities stopped in order to begin teaching trials. If the latter situation develops, the learner may resist the teaching trials because they are accompanied by termination of immediately ongoing, preferred events.

If teaching trials always immediately follow the antecedent events, and such events are brief, then any problems with a learner not wanting to discontinue the activities to participate in the teaching session are usually short-lived. The learner comes to realize that the antecedent events are setting the occasion for teaching trials. When the other components of the *Preferred ABC Model* are appropriately carried out as discussed in the remainder of this and subsequent chapters, the learner becomes aware that the antecedent events are a signal for an immediately forthcoming, enjoyable activity.

> **Environmental changes and events occurring before a teaching session should lead directly into actual teaching trials without any break in time; the antecedent events should be a signal to the learner that another enjoyable activity is immediately forthcoming.**

Enjoyable Activities Associated With Teacher And Learner Behavior During A Teaching Session

Within the *"Behavior"* or *B* part of the *Preferred ABC Model* there are two sets of organizational procedures for enhancing learner enjoyment with a teaching session. The first set involves providing preferred items and activities while the actual teaching session is taking place. The second set of procedures pertains to providing brief breaks from instructional trials if the learner's behavior suggests discontent or unhappiness.

Providing Enjoyable Items and Activities During Teaching

Learner enjoyment during teaching can be enhanced if preferred items and activities are provided for the learner periodically during a teaching session. Presentation of preferred items and activities should be a part of the teacher's instructional behavior.

The most common way to provide preferred items and activities is between instructional trials. Many teaching sessions with people who have developmental disabilities involve several instructional trials with the task-analyzed skill being taught. That is, the learner is prompted through the complete task analysis for one trial, and then the process is repeated a set number of times. Once a trial is completed, a preferred item or activity can be provided briefly before initiating the next trial.

Another way in which preferred items and activities can be provided during a teaching session is when there is only one trial with a particular skill during a teaching session but the skill involves a large number of task-analyzed steps. For example, a program to teach an individual in a supported living arrangement to clean the living room may involve upward of 20 steps related to such things as dusting flat surfaces, wiping blinds, organizing magazines on a table, emptying a trash can, vacuuming the floor, etc. When there is a large number of task-analyzed steps to complete, preferred items and activities can be provided periodically between certain steps in the task analysis. To maintain continuity in the instructional process, it is generally best to provide the items and activities when there is a natural break between steps (e.g., when all the dusting has been completed and the next step in the task analysis involves a different cleaning duty such as beginning to vacuum).

Before elaborating on how preferred items and activities can be provided within an ongoing teaching session, one situation in which this particular procedure associated with the *Preferred ABC Model* should not be conducted warrants mention. For individuals with very profound disabilities, some teaching sessions involve only one or a very small number of instructional trials and task-analyzed steps. To illustrate, teaching a person with profound cognitive disabilities and serious motor impairment to press a pressure plate switch to activate a CD player may only involve the steps of moving the hand to the switch and pressing down on the switch. Further, it may be determined that the learner can only cope with one trial of going through the two steps within a given teaching session due to fatigue. When there is only a small number of trials and steps comprising a teaching session, generally it is best not to provide preferred items or activities between the task-analyzed steps.

In the situation just noted, providing preferred items and activities during the teaching session is likely to interfere with the instructional process. However, the other set of procedures constituting the *B* component of the *Preferred ABC Model* – that of taking a brief break when a learner's behavior suggests discontent – should still be conducted as discussed in the next section. Procedures comprising the *A* and *C* components of the *Model* for enhancing learner enjoyment with a teaching session should also be provided.

During an actual teaching session, provision of preferred *items* for a learner is generally most successful with learners who have more severe disabilities. In contrast, provision of preferred *activities* usually can be successfully provided with learners with all levels of disabilities. For the former individuals, often only one preferred item is needed to enhance enjoyment with the teaching session, although different items can also be provided within a session. Some of the items we have seen used to increase enjoyment that a learner with profound disabilities experiences during a teaching session include:

- **Giving a child a favorite toy to hold or play with**
- **Giving a learner a piece of a favorite snack item**
- **Giving a learner a small vibrator to hold next to his cheek**
- **Giving a child an animal sticker to place on a worksheet**
- **Giving a learner a favorite picture to look at**

When providing preferred items to enhance enjoyment during a teaching session, care should be taken to provide only items that can be enjoyed when accessed briefly by the learner. Items should be avoided that may continuously captivate a learner's attention for extended time periods such that the learner cannot be easily re-directed back to the teacher's instructions. To maintain continuity with the instructional process, items provided between instructional trials or steps of a task analysis have to be removed after a few seconds. If an item requires several minutes or more to enjoy, such as playing with a hand-held computer game, then it can be problematic to stop the learner's engagement with the item in order to continue teaching trials.

It is also important to begin the instructional process immediately after the item is removed from the learner. Engagement with the item should be viewed as part of the instructional process and not a separate activity per se in order to maintain the flow and expediency of instruction. This is why use of preferred items and activities is considered part of the teacher's instructional behavior within the *Preferred ABC Model*. The overall process should involve one or more instructional trials immediately followed by an opportunity for the learner to engage with a preferred item, and then immediately followed by re-initiation of instructional trials. If breaks in time occur between the learner's engagement with the preferred item and instructional trials, engaging with the item may be viewed by the learner as a distinct activity. When the latter situation occurs, it can become difficult to re-direct the learner's attention back to instructional trials.

Providing preferred activities during a teaching session occurs in basically the same way as provision of preferred items. In this case though, instead of the teacher providing the learner with access to a preferred item, the teacher conducts an activity with the learner that the learner enjoys. As noted earlier, whereas providing a preferred item to engage with is most applicable with learners who have more severe disabilities, providing preferred activities is usually applicable with learners of all severities of disabilities.

Similar to presentation of preferred items during teaching sessions, preferred activities presented during a teaching session should be brief in nature, and be followed immediately by re-initiation of instructional trials. Types of preferred activities that can be provided are highly varied, depending on individual learner preferences. Often, very simple activities can be conducted briefly such as talking to a learner about something the learner enjoys or joking with the learner. Some of the activities we have found helpful to include during teaching sessions with different learners to enhance enjoyment include:

- **Providing a stretch or movement break**
- **Massaging the learner's shoulders or arms**
- **Providing an opportunity to watch other people doing things in the immediate environment**
- **Giving a brief rest period with no activity**

Another means of incorporating preferred activities within a teaching session pertains more directly to the teaching trials than the examples just provided. With some learners, providing occasional teaching trials on tasks that the learners already know how to perform can make a teaching session more enjoyable. For example, when teaching a learner how to recognize various information symbols in public places, trials involving symbols the learner has already learned how to identify can be interspersed with trials the learner is learning to identify. In this manner, *easier* instructional tasks are interspersed with more *difficult* tasks.

Interspersing easier tasks with more difficult tasks is particularly advantageous for learners who are highly motivated to learn and become displeased when they know they have performed incorrectly or are having difficulty with particular tasks. By interspersing easier tasks within the teaching process, the learner has more opportunities to experience success. Such success helps make the learning process more enjoyable for the learner.

> **A teaching program can become more enjoyable for a learner if tasks that are easy for the learner to perform are interspersed among tasks that are more difficult to perform.**

Interspersing easy tasks among more difficult tasks is not only a good means of making the teaching process more enjoyable for many learners, the process also enhances the effectiveness of teaching. Teaching effectiveness is enhanced in part because interspersing previously learned tasks provides a review of previous learning, which helps maintain the learner's previously acquired skills. Additionally, because the learner is likely to respond correctly to the easier tasks provided occasionally during a teaching session relative to tasks that have not yet been learned, responses to the easier tasks provide more opportunities for the teacher to reinforce correct performance. Such reinforcement can increase the likelihood the learner will continue to respond to subsequent teacher instructions.

Providing a Brief Break Following Signs of Learner Discontent

When the procedures described throughout this text are used by teachers, learner discontent with a teaching program is usually short lived. Nevertheless, teachers must be prepared to respond to learner behavior that indicates discontent. Teacher preparation in this regard is especially important for learners who previously have shown active dislike of participating in teaching programs. The second set of procedures within the *Behavior (B)* part of the *Preferred ABC Model* directly addresses learner discontent that may arise. These steps involve providing a brief break from teaching upon any learner behavior suggesting discontent, followed immediately by presentation of a brief preferred item or activity, followed in turn by immediately resuming the teaching at the point that it was temporarily discontinued. This process is illustrated in the following diagram.

Learner's behavior suggests discontent

↓

Teacher provides brief break and preferred activity

↓

Teacher returns to instruction where break occurred, prompts learner to complete instructional trial

---

In order to implement this part of the *Preferred ABC Model*, the teacher must be able to quickly identify behavior suggesting discontent on the part of the learner. For some learners, such behavior is readily apparent in that they will become physically disruptive, aggressive, or engage in self-injurious behavior. For other learners though, discontent is more subtle. The latter learners may, for example, simply sit and do nothing, begin to engage in stereotypic behavior, or attempt to engage the teacher in a conversation or activity unrelated to the teaching task.

Being able to quickly identify behavior indicating learner discontent is another reason why it is important that a teacher spend time establishing a relationship and getting to know a learner prior to implementing a teaching program. A natural outcome of spending time with a potential learner is that as the teacher becomes familiar with how the learner communicates, the teacher will also become knowledgeable about the learner's behavior that reflects discontent with something.

Once discontent is shown by a learner during a teaching program, the teacher should quickly stop the instruction and provide a brief break from the teaching by helping the learner do something that is enjoyable. It is important to immediately respond to behavior suggesting discontent because generally, the longer a learner is discontented the harder it is to overcome the discontent. The same types of preferred items and activities that were described earlier for presentation between instructional trials can be presented upon signs of discontent as a means of engaging the learner in something enjoyable. Again though, the break from the teaching and presentation of preferred items or activities should be very brief, lasting no more than a few minutes at most. Subsequently, immediately afterwards the teacher should resume instruction at the exact place that it was discontinued when the discontent was first noticed.

Returning to the exact place in the instructional sequence at which discontent by the learner was first observed is a critical step in the overall process of making teaching effective and enjoyable. If the teacher does not return to the original place, the learner could learn that certain parts of teaching programs can be avoided or terminated by acting out. That is, a learner may learn to engage in behavior that appears to show discontent as a means of getting the teacher to stop that part of the teaching process. If the teacher always returns to the point at which discontent was first observed and then requires the learner to complete that part of the teaching task (e.g., through least-to-most helpful prompting as discussed in **Chapter 3**), the learner will quickly become aware that "faking" discontent will not result in escape from respective instructional tasks.

> **Brief breaks from teaching and presentation of preferred items or activities upon signs of learner discontent should always be followed by a return to the point in the teaching process at which the discontent was first observed.**

When implementing this part of the *B* component of the *Preferred ABC Model*, a point of caution is warranted. After providing brief breaks and a preferred item or activity a few times, some learners may engage in behavior suggesting discontent not because they are displeased with a respective teaching procedure but because they like the breaks and ensuing item or activity that follow such behavior. Relatedly, some learners may engage in behavior typically characteristic of discontent because they like interacting with the teacher. They begin to realize that by displaying such behavior, the duration of the teaching process and therefore their individualized time with the teacher can be extended (i.e., by the added breaks following signs of discontent). This development will become apparent if a learner begins to increase how often discontent is displayed once a teacher begins to follow the behavior with a brief break and preferred item or activity.

If the situations just described are observed, then behavior suggesting discontent should no longer be followed by any break from the teaching process. Preferred items or activities should be presented only following specific instructional trials as described previously. Generally however, learners will not purposely increase their signs of discontent if the *Consequence* part of the *Preferred ABC Model* is appropriately carried out by the teacher.

Conducting Enjoyable Activities As A Consequence To A Teaching Session

The primary intent of the *Consequence (C)* component of the *Preferred ABC* approach is to follow every teaching program with something the learner really likes. A very enjoyable item and/or activity should be provided immediately after a teaching session is completed. Attempts should be made to provide the learner's most preferred thing to do after the teaching session is over. Ways to identify items and activities that are highly preferred by a learner, and therefore help the learner have an enjoyable time after a teaching session, are described in **Chapter 8**. Of course, the more familiar a teacher is with a given learner as discussed repeatedly already, the more likely it is that the teacher will be able to identify things a learner really likes to do after a teaching session.

In contrast to providing enjoyable items and activities before and during teaching sessions, the presentation of enjoyable events after a teaching session does not have to be brief. Rather, the item or activity should be presented for as long as is necessary for the learner to experience significant enjoyment. Some of the things we have found to present to a learner as a consequence to a teaching session that were highly desired by the learner include the following:

- **Swinging in a hammock**
- **Putting on make-up**
- **Playing with favorite toys**

- **Having general free time in a classroom**
- **Receiving a favorite snack**
- **Playing a game with the teacher or classmates**

When planning what to provide as a consequence to a teaching session, confusion sometimes arises regarding how this component of the *Preferred ABC Model* coincides with the reinforcement part of teaching as discussed in **Chapter 3.** To review briefly, a critical part of making teaching effective is to provide a reinforcer following the learner's correct completion of the last step in the program task analysis. Reinforcing the last correctly completed step in the task analysis is crucial for increasing the likelihood that the learner will continue to attempt to learn and perform the skill being taught. In contrast, the consequence part of the teaching process discussed here is intended to make the overall teaching program enjoyable for the learner. The item or activity that is provided after the teaching program should follow presentation of the reinforcer for the task completion.

In actuality, the effects of the reinforcer provided following the learner's skill completion (which is usually teacher praise) and the effects of the subsequent preferred activity can overlap. Providing a reinforcing event for correct skill completion can make teaching more enjoyable, and the following preferred item or activity can serve the purpose of reinforcing skill completion. Hence, the two procedures are complimentary. Due to timing of presentation and other factors related to principles of learning though, the effects of the two procedures do not always overlap. Therefore, both procedures should be included within teaching programs to help ensure the programs are both effective and enjoyable for the learner.

> **A reinforcer should be provided immediately after the correct completion of the last step in the task analysis; a highly preferred item or activity should then be provided at the conclusion of the teaching session.**

When a teacher consistently follows a teaching session with an item or event that a learner finds truly enjoyable, two beneficial outcomes result. First, the initiation of a teaching session signals to the learner that an enjoyable experience is forthcoming – the learner knows that as soon as the teaching session is completed, good things will happen. This sets the occasion for the learner to look forward to the teacher's instructional program. Second, a learner will often increase efforts to complete instructional trials correctly in order to finish the teaching session as soon as possible in order to begin the enjoyable activity. These two outcomes, when coupled with the *Antecedent* and *Behavior* components of the *Preferred ABC Model*, can seriously increase motivation to learn skills being taught within teaching sessions as well as enhance learner enjoyment with the overall teaching process.

Chapter Review Questions

1. The Preferred ABC Model refers to what three time segments associated with carrying out a teaching program?

2. What are two general approaches that can be conducted before a teaching session to enhance learner enjoyment and responsiveness during the teaching session?

3. How can events be interspersed among teaching trials to enhance learner enjoyment?

4. How should a brief break from instruction be conducted to reduce learner discontent without inadvertently causing signs of discontent to increase?

5. What type of preferred activity should be provided immediately after a teaching session to enhance learner enjoyment?

Chapter 7

Building Choice Into Teaching Programs

The preceding chapter discussed how teaching sessions should be organized from a general perspective to make teaching programs enjoyable for the learner. It was emphasized that enjoyable items or events should be presented as antecedents to a teaching session, in association with teacher and learner behavior during the session, and as a consequence to the session. This chapter focuses on one type of event that can be particularly helpful to provide as part of the antecedent and consequence activities of a teaching program: learner *choice*.

Beginning in the 1990s, increased attention was directed to providing more choice in the lives of people with developmental disabilities. Efforts to increase choice opportunities occurred for several reasons. On a basic level, it was recognized that individual choice is a fundamental right of all people, and exercising that right has a tremendous impact on one's quality of life. The more choice a person has on a day-to-day basis, generally the more enjoyment the person experiences. However, it also was recognized that relative to the general populace, people with developmental disabilities -- and especially severe disabilities – often had few choice-making opportunities during their daily routines.

As recognition grew regarding the lack of choice in the lives of many people with developmental disabilities, a considerable amount of behavioral research focused on means of increasing choice opportunities. As specific ways to provide more choices were developed, it became apparent that by increasing choice making, people with severe disabilities experienced many desirable outcomes. Some of the more noted benefits of providing frequent choice opportunities during day-to-day activities include:

- **Increased enjoyment with daily living**
- **Reduced occurrence of problem behavior**
- **More active and varied leisure pursuits**
- **More productive work performance**

Perhaps the best way to grasp the importance of increased choice making in the lives of people with developmental disabilities is to consider *individual control*. When an individual makes a choice about something, that person is exerting control. People like to have control over their lives whether they have disabilities or not. Having control allows an individual to live in accordance with the individual's personal likes and dislikes.

When opportunities to make choices are lacking, then an individual's personal control is diminished. For people with severe disabilities, that control usually is assumed by support personnel. Consequently, when choice-making opportunities are lacking, individuals with severe disabilities tend to live their lives in accordance with the preferences of support personnel instead of their own likes and dislikes.

> **Making choices allows people with severe disabilities to have control over their lives, and to live their lives in accordance with their personal likes and dislikes.**

Because of the importance choice has on a person's daily enjoyment, building choice-making opportunities into teaching programs represents a highly effective means of increasing a learner's enjoyment with the programs. Hence, choice should be a regular part of the teaching process. Choice can be incorporated within teaching programs most easily by providing choice opportunities as part of the antecedent and consequence components of teaching sessions.

Prior to describing ways to provide various choice opportunities before and after teaching sessions, it is important to focus on *how* specific choices should be presented. To represent a true choice-making opportunity, a choice must be provided in a way that a learner can understand and respond to with a valid choice. Because of the varied cognitive and communication challenges of learners with severe disabilities, some learners can respond to certain types of choice opportunities whereas other learners lack the skills to understand and respond to those particular opportunities. Special care must be taken by teachers to provide choice-making opportunities for learners that are commensurate with the learners' cognitive and communication skills.

Providing Choice-Making Opportunities In Accordance With A Learner's Skill Level

As just indicated, for a teacher's choice presentation to be meaningful for a learner, the learner must be able to understand what is being offered and respond with a functional choice. In turn, the teacher must know how to provide the choice in a way that the learner understands, and how to recognize the learner's choice response.

If the pre-requisites for making a teaching program enjoyable for a learner have been adhered to as described earlier, a teacher usually will have a good idea about providing choices in a way the learner can understand. Most important in this regard is that the teacher must have established a good relationship with the learner. As stressed repeatedly, establishing a good relationship involves the teacher spending time with a learner to help the learner enjoy interacting with the teacher. Spending time with the learner in this manner usually familiarizes the teacher with the learner's idiosyncratic communication skills. Such familiarity is critical to determining how to provide a meaningful choice opportunity for the learner

Even when a teacher is well familiar with a learner and has established a good relationship, it can be beneficial if the teacher attempts several different ways of providing choices. The intent is to ensure that as part of the teaching program, choices are presented in a way that best coincides with the learner's receptive and expressive skills. The following sections describe the most useful strategies for providing choices in a meaningful manner to learners with severe disabilities and varying communication challenges.

The Most Useful Choice-Presentation Strategy

The most useful choice-presentation strategy for learners with severe disabilities is typically a *paired-item* choice. In the paired-item method of providing a choice, a learner is presented with two items from which to choose one item. The items can be things that the learner will use directly, such as two different snacks or drinks to consume, two different types of work materials to use, or two toys with which to play. The items can also serve as referents to different activities in which a learner can choose to participate. That is, the items can represent choices of activities. To illustrate, a CD and a basketball may be presented to indicate that a learner can choose to listen to music on a CD player or shoot baskets.

The paired-item format is generally considered the most useful means of providing choices because it is the strategy that most learners with severe disabilities can readily understand and respond to in a meaningful manner. The following diagram illustrates the basic process for providing a paired-item choice.

Paired-Item Choice-Presentation Format

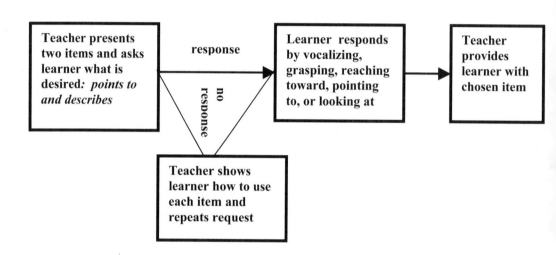

As indicated in the illustration, a teacher provides a paired-item choice by presenting two items within arm's reach of a learner and asking the learner which of the items is desired. When the teacher asks what is desired, the teacher also points to and briefly describes each item to the learner to enhance the likelihood the learner understands what is presented. If the teacher is not sure at this point that the learner understands what is being presented, the teacher may need to show the learner how to use each item or assist the learner in briefly using each item, and then re-present the two items in the manner just described. Next, the teacher waits for the learner to indicate a choice by vocalizing, grasping or reaching toward an item, pointing to an item or in some cases (e.g., for learners with serious physical disabilities) looking at an item for several seconds. Once the learner indicates which item is desired with a choice response, the teacher then provides the learner with the item or begins the activity that the item represents.

In most cases, if the teacher is familiar with a learner's likes and dislikes (see **Chapter 8** for additional information on how to assess learner preferences) and involves preferred items or activities in the choice presentation, a learner will choose one of the presented items. At times though, a choice response will not be apparent. The learner may not make a choice, for example, due to a lack of interest in either item at that particular moment. When a learner does not make an apparent choice, the teacher can present other items for choice or discontinue the choice presentation at that point in time and then repeat it later.

> **The paired-item method represents a way of providing choices that is most frequently understood by most people who have severe disabilities.**

Choice-Presentation Strategies for Learners with More Advanced Communication Skills

For some learners with severe disabilities it is not necessary to show two items as part of the paired-item method. Some learners can readily understand a choice opportunity if the teacher vocally describes what the two choice options are for the learner, and then asks the learner which option is desired (or provides the description through manual signing or a related gestural strategy). This format is useful for learners with good receptive communication skills. However, when a choice is presented in this manner, the learner also must have the expressive skills to vocalize which option is desired (or use an available augmentative communication means to make a choice response).

For other learners, their communication challenges may be too significant to allow understanding and responding to a vocal description of two choice options, but may be able to respond to pictorial representations of items or activities. For these learners, the teacher can present pictures of items or activities in the same manner as described when presenting actual items. This process is also advantageous for learners who use augmentative devices for communication purposes. With the latter individuals, the teacher can use pictures or symbols within the learner's device for presenting choices of two items or activities.

Choice-Presentation Strategies for Learners with Less Advanced Communication Skills

For learners with the most significant disabilities, such as profound multiple disabilities, even the paired-item choice process can be too difficult. For these individuals, sometimes one item has to be presented at a time by presenting the item within arm's reach of the learner and describing the item or activity it represents. The teacher may also have to assist the learner in briefly using the item or participating in the activity the item represents to enhance the learner's understanding of what is presented. The teacher then waits to see if the learner approaches the item in any way (see earlier description of how learners may choose an item). After one item is presented briefly, the teacher presents another item and observes for an approach response. The teacher then evaluates the learner's responses to the two items and determines which one appeared to be approached more actively by the learner.

Special Considerations in Determining A Choice-Presentation Strategy

At times a teacher will have to provide choices to a learner in two or more of the ways just described to determine the particular way that is most meaningful for a learner. The **Providing Choice Opportunities** section of the **Selected Readings** lists a number of references to sources that provide in-depth discussions of how to present choice opportunities for learners with severe disabilities who tend to experience difficulty in making choices. There are also two special considerations that warrant attention when determining the most advantageous way to provide a choice to a learner with severe disabilities. These considerations include what to do if a learner does not make a choice following a choice presentation by the teacher, and limiting choices to two items or activities.

What To Do If A Learner Does Not Make A Choice

When discussing the paired-item choice process, it was noted that sometimes a learner will not respond to the choice presentation with an apparent choice response. It was also noted that when a learner does not make a choice response, the teacher should present other choice options or wait a little while and present the choice again. This same strategy for what to do when a learner does not respond to a paired-item choice is useful when learners do not respond to the other choice-presentation strategies just described.

If a learner consistently fails to make a choice response despite repeated choice presentations involving different items or activities, it is likely that the learner does not understand the way choices are being presented. In such cases, the teacher should provide choices in ways that are easier to understand. The choice presentation strategies described under the previous chapter section for learners with more advanced communication skills are generally the most difficult for learners to understand; the method described in the section pertaining to learners with less advanced communication skills is generally the easiest for learners to understand.

Type of Choice Presentation and Difficulty Level for Learner Choice Response

Type of choice	Learner difficulty
vocal	hard
paired item	moderate
single item	easy

Limiting Choices to Two Items or Activities

The discussion on choice-presentation strategies has focused on choices of two items or activities. There are also a number of ways to provide choices of three or more items or activities (again see **Providing Choice Opportunities** in the **Selected Readings**). However, it is recommended that when incorporating choices into teaching programs, the choices generally be limited to two items or activities.

Limiting choices to two items or activities is necessary for practical reasons. As indicated in **Chapter 6**, strategies for incorporating enjoyment into teaching programs should be conducted relatively quickly. Procedures to enhance enjoyment should be conducted quickly to prevent the activities from interfering with actual teaching of skills to the learner. Typically, choices involving more than two items and activities involve more time on the part of the learner to process the choice presentations and respond to the choice opportunities. Limiting the choices to two items or activities reduces the likelihood that the choice presentations and responses will interfere with the teaching process. Limiting choices in this manner also reduces the time and effort on the part of the teacher to plan and then conduct a teaching session.

Providing Choices As Antecedents And Consequences To A Teaching Session

Earlier it was noted that to enhance learner enjoyment with a teaching program, choices should be provided as part of the antecedent and consequence components of a teaching session. In most cases, it is too cumbersome to provide learner choices *during* actual implementation of a teaching program. Attempting to provide choices while teaching trials are being presented also can interfere significantly with the teaching process. Nonetheless, if choices are provided before and after implementation of the teaching program, such choices significantly enhance learner enjoyment with the overall teaching session. Preceding and following implementation of a teaching program with learner choices can also prevent problem behavior that would otherwise be likely with some learners when a teacher attempts to carry out an instructional program.

> **Providing learner choices immediately before and after a teaching program is carried out can enhance learner enjoyment with the program and reduce the likelihood of problem behavior.**

The following sections describe ways in which learner choices can be provided before and after a teaching program is implemented. Again though, the choices must be provided in a way that the learner can readily understand and respond to with a recognizable choice. It is also important to note that not all the ways to provide choices to be described can be incorporated within each teaching session. It is usually too time consuming to provide a variety of choices before and after each session;

attempting to provide too many choices is impractical for most teaching situations.

Teachers should decide which choices appear most important to a learner, and which choices are easiest to provide before and after a teaching session. A useful guideline is to attempt to provide one choice before a session and one choice after a session. If additional choices can be provided without requiring too much time or preparation on the part of the teacher, then those choices could also be provided.

> **Teachers should strive to provide one choice immediately before a teaching program is implemented and one choice immediately after the program has been completed.**

Providing Choices As An Antecedent To A Teaching Program

Providing a choice to a learner as an antecedent to a teaching program helps set the occasion for the program to be well received by the learner. Giving the learner a choice increases the likelihood that a specific way in which at least part of the teaching process is carried out is something the learner prefers – when people make a choice, they usually choose what they prefer. In this case, the learner is choosing something that the learner wants to occur as part of the teaching program relative to something the learner does not want, or does not want as much.

Providing a choice immediately before a teaching session also can be an effective means of preventing behavior problems during the teaching session for certain learners. Some learners like to be in control of various things. When the learners perceive that they do not have control, they may resort to problem behavior in an attempt to acquire control or to avoid the situation in which they do not have control. When the learners are provided a choice in regard to how some aspect of the teaching program will be carried out, the learners are exerting a degree of control over the teaching process. As such, behavior problems that arise when a learner perceives a lack of control can be avoided or minimized.

There are many different choices that can be provided as an antecedent to a teaching session. To facilitate a teacher's determination of particular choices to present when planning a teaching session, it can be helpful to consider four basic types of choices. These include:

- ***What* choices**
- ***How* choices**
- ***Where* choices**
- ***When* choices**

The first type of choice pertains to *what* will be done by the learner. When planning a teaching session, these types of choices usually pertain to what teaching program will be conducted. At times, a teacher can let the learner choose which of two teaching programs will take place (e.g., "Do you want to work on your money program or your writing program?"). Of course, what is taught at a given point will not always be open for negotiation. Some programs have to be carried out at certain times or in certain locations. It is the teacher's responsibility to decide if respective programs have to be carried out at a certain time or if the programs could be carried out later if the learner chooses not to work on a given program at the moment.

The second type of choice, the *how* choices, usually allow more flexibility on the part of the teacher than *what* choices. These types of choices pertain to how some aspect of the teaching program will be carried out. To illustrate, if a program involves teaching name writing to a learner, the learner could be given a choice of writing with a pen or a pencil, or with a blue marker or red marker. In this way, teaching trials are carried out in the same manner by the teacher for instructional purposes, but how the learner responds to the trials can be based on the learner's preference (e.g., with the pen versus the pencil or with the blue marker versus the red marker). Examples of ways teachers have incorporated *how* choices when initiating a teaching session are provided below.

- **Giving a choice to a learner to complete a collating task by standing next to a table or sitting at the table**
- **Allowing a learner to choose to fold his socks first or his shorts first as part of an instructional program on laundry skills**
- **Providing a learner a choice of counting with pennies or counting with cards**
- **Giving a choice of cooking vegetable soup or chicken noodle soup as part of a program to teach use of**

- the microwave
- **Providing a choice of using the red or blue pressure plate switch as part of a program to teach a learner how to maintain pressure on a switch to activate a CD player**

In considering examples of *how* choices as just presented, it becomes apparent that some *how* choices are likely to be more important to a learner than other *how* choices. To illustrate, choosing what to cook and subsequently eat in conjunction with a cooking program would seem to be more important in most situations than choosing the color of a pencil to use in a writing program. Generally, the more important the choice to the learner, the more the choice enhances learner enjoyment with the program.

Even when a choice opportunity may not appear at first glance to be particularly important, it can still be useful to provide the choice before a teaching program if that is the only choice that can be arranged. Sometimes the act of choosing itself can enhance a learner's enjoyment; choosing can be a preferred activity. Additionally, making a choice can provide a learner with a degree of control over the teaching session. As noted earlier, exerting control represents a desired situation for many learners.

> **The act of choosing itself can be an enjoyable event for a learner.**

The third type of choice that can be provided before a teaching session is a *where* choice. Sometimes a learner can be provided a choice of where a teaching program will be conducted, or where parts of the program will be conducted. A special needs student may be given a choice, for example, of working on a money recognition program at the student's desk or at the teacher's desk. An individual in a group home may be given a choice of working on a program to teach how to use a DVD player in the living room or in the learner's bedroom (assuming there is a DVD player in both locations).

Providing a choice of where a learner will participate in a teaching program can make the program more enjoyable when a learner prefers a certain location over another. Of course, the location in which some teaching programs need to be conducted cannot be altered due to the nature of the programs, such as being taught how to clean tables in a school cafeteria as part of a vocational training program. For many programs though, the location is not especially important. For the latter types of programs, teachers should give consideration to offering a learner a choice of where the program will occur and particularly if the teacher is aware that a learner prefers some locations over others.

The final type of choice to be considered in planning a teaching session is a *when* choice. A variation on *when* choices was discussed previously in regard to *what* choices. To review briefly, *what* choices involve giving a learner a choice of working on one of two tasks now and the other task later. Hence, this type of choice also involves when a given program will be implemented. Other types of *when* choices pertain simply to when one specific program will be conducted (e.g., "Do you want to practice using the dishwasher after lunch or after supper?").

As with other types of choices, *when* choices are not appropriate for every teaching program. Some skills need to be taught at specific times, such as how to clean up after a meal. However, many other programs can be conducted at various times during the day, such that a teacher can consider giving the learner a choice of when to participate in the program.

One word of caution is in order when considering *when* choices. Generally, giving a choice to a learner of when a teaching session will take place should only occur one time per day. For some learners, if they are given a choice of when a teaching session will occur several times during the day, they may learn that they can keep putting off a session or avoid it altogether. In the latter cases, learners can be resistive to participating in a program when, after having chosen not to participate in the program several times, the teacher directs the learner to participate in the program because it cannot be delayed any longer.

Providing Choices As A Consequence To A Teaching Program

As discussed in **Chapter 6**, immediately after a teaching program is completed the teacher should involve the learner in something that is highly desired by the learner. A good means of ensuring that what is provided as a consequence to the teaching session is truly desired by the learner is to provide the learner with a choice of what to do. Hence, the most important choice to be provided after a teaching session is a *what* choice.

For learners with more advanced communication and cognitive skills, the choice of what to do when a teaching program is completed can be provided prior to beginning the teaching session. For example, a learner may be asked, "What would you like to do after we finish working on learning how to wash your clothes? Would you like to sit on the patio or watch television?". Once the teaching session is completed, the teacher then supports the learner in doing what was chosen at the beginning of the session.

Choices of what to do after a teaching session, whether decided at the beginning of a session by more advanced learners or immediately after a session by learners who are less advanced communicatively, should involve choices between two highly preferred items or activities. Learner enjoyment with a teaching session is maximized when a learner knows that something highly desired will happen as soon as the program is completed. Choices between two strongly preferred items or activities typically are more desirable to a learner than choices involving only one highly preferred option and an option that is noticeably less preferred by the learner.

> **Immediately after completing a teaching session, a teacher should offer the learner a choice between two items or activities that are highly preferred by the learner.**

In order to provide choices of highly preferred things to do after a teaching session, a teacher must be well familiar with a learner's most preferred items and activities. The likelihood of a teacher having a good familiarity of a learner's strongest preferences is enhanced considerably if the teacher has taken the time to establish a good relationship with the learner. For many learners though, and particularly those with the most severe disabilities, establishing a good relationship is only part of what is necessary to make sure a teacher is familiar with a learner's preferences. For the latter individuals, more systematic steps usually must be taken to determine their preferences. **Chapter 8** provides additional information on how to accurately identify learner preferences.

Chapter Review Questions

1. What are four beneficial effects of providing choices to learners with developmental disabilities?

2. How does a learner's skill level affect how a choice opportunity should be provided by a teacher?

3. How is a paired-item choice presentation made?

4. For learners with relatively advanced communication skills, what is an alternative to the paired-item method of presenting a choice?

5. How is a one-item choice presentation made?

6. Generally, how many items or activities should be involved in choices offered in association with a teaching session?

7. With respect to the Preferred ABC Model, in what two components should choices be provided?

8. What are four basic types of choices?

9. In regard to a learner's preferences, what should be included in choices offered after a teaching session?

Chapter 8

Positive Reinforcers and Preferred Events

An integral aspect of making teaching both effective and enjoyable for learners with disabilities is the use of positive reinforcers and preferred events. As discussed in **Chapter 3**, a *positive reinforcer* is something a teacher provides following a learner's response to an instructional trial that makes it more likely the learner will continue to respond to teaching trials. The learner will respond to future instructional trials to obtain the reinforcer.

> **A positive reinforcer is an item or activity provided by a teacher following a learner's response to an instructional trial that makes it more likely the learner will continue to respond to instructional trials.**

Preferred events refer to items and activities that a learner likes. A positive reinforcer represents one type of preferred event. However, all preferred events are not reinforcers. A learner may like something, but not like it enough to work for it. In the context of a teaching session, a preferred event functions as a reinforcer only when a learner will work to obtain the item or activity by responding in the correct manner to an instructional trial.

Differentiating between preferred events that represent reinforcers versus those that are not reinforcers even though they are liked by a learner may seem like an overly academic distinction. The distinction is important though when attempting to ensure both the effectiveness and enjoyment of a teaching session. Both types of events contribute to teaching effectiveness and learner enjoyment, but in different ways.

> **Preferred events refer to items and activities that a learner likes; positive reinforcers are certain types of preferred events that a learner will work to obtain.**

A Review of Providing Reinforcement During Teaching

It was noted in **Chapter 3** that a teacher should always provide a positive reinforcer following the learner's completion of the last step in the task analysis of the skill being taught. In this manner, the learner will be motivated to work through the steps in the task analysis to obtain the reinforcer following the last step. Because a reinforcer is a type of preferred event as just described, providing a reinforcer following the last completed step in the task analysis also helps the learner enjoy the teaching session -- the learner experiences an enjoyable event associated with completing the session.

As also discussed in **Chapter 3**, the most readily available and efficient reinforcer to motivate learner responses during teaching is praise from the teacher. However, a given teacher's praise may not automatically function as a reinforcer. Teachers must take the time and effort to establish a good rapport with the learner (**Chapter 5**) to ensure their praise is something a learner will work to obtain during teaching sessions.

Although the most important time to provide praise as a reinforcer for learner responding during a teaching session is following the learner's completion of the last step in the task analysis, it can also be important to provide praise at other times. Praise can be provided for steps in the task analysis prior to the last step that the learner completes correctly, as well as for learner attempts to complete various steps even if the learner needs help to perform the steps. Providing praise -- which is usually one type of preferred event -- periodically during teaching trials in this manner can help maintain a learner's motivation to learn the skill being taught, as well as enhance learner enjoyment with the teaching.

Providing Preferred Events

The primary reason positive reinforcement is provided during teaching is to motivate a learner to respond to instructional trials. A secondary effect is enhancement of learner enjoyment with the teaching process as just summarized. Preferred events that do not necessarily represent reinforcers but are nonetheless liked by a learner should also be provided during teaching sessions. The primary purpose of the latter types of preferred events is not to reinforce responding to instructional trials per se, but to enhance learner enjoyment with the overall teaching process. Providing preferred events within the context of the *Antecedent, Behavior, Consequence (ABC) Model of Preference-Based Teaching* (**Chapter 6**) is a powerful means of helping a learner enjoy teaching sessions.

One method of providing preferred events as part of the teaching process is to provide choices before and after a teaching session as described in **Chapter 7**. When a learner makes a choice associated with a teaching session, the learner will access a preferred item or activity. By definition, the act of choosing means that an individual selects one item or activity that is more preferred over the alternative item or activity that is presented for choice.

In addition to giving choice opportunities between items or activities, a teacher can select one preferred item or activity and present it to the learner. A primary advantage of the teacher selecting the preferred item or activity for the learner in contrast to having the learner choose between two items or activities is that the former process takes less time. Providing a choice by presenting two items or activity referents in a manner that the learner can understand and respond to involves several steps (again, see **Chapter** 7). In contrast, providing one preferred item or activity takes only one step. Additionally, there is less time involved for the learner to begin to engage with a teacher-presented, preferred item or activity relative to the time involved for the learner to process a choice presentation and make a selection.

Another advantage of providing preferred items and activities relative to providing a choice is that at times, it is difficult for a teacher to identify two options to present for a choice. This difficulty arises most often with people who have more severe disabilities, and for whom it can be difficult to identify different preferred items or activities to include in a choice opportunity. In some cases, there is only one clearly identified item or activity that is preferred by a respective learner that can be readily presented during the teaching process.

Although there are advantages of a teacher giving a learner a preferred item or activity relative to presenting a choice opportunity, choices should still be provided when possible. Most advantageously, preferred items and activities should be provided as part of the teaching process along with choices offered before and after a teaching session.

> **Learner enjoyment with a teaching session is maximally enhanced if the teacher provides choice opportunities before and after a teaching session, and provides preferred items and activities during the actual teaching session.**

Providing preferred items and activities requires the teacher to be knowledgeable about a learner's preferences. In some cases, learner preferences are readily apparent to teachers. In other cases, and particularly with learners who have more severe disabilities, items and activities the learners prefer are not always apparent.

Ways to Identify Learner Preferences

A considerable amount of research has occurred on ways of identifying preferences among people who have severe disabilities. Researchers have focused on preference identification for two reasons. First, the importance of identifying preferred events for individuals with severe disabilities has become well recognized. A person's quality of life is enhanced immeasurably if the individual has access to things that are liked or preferred. In order to support people with severe disabilities in accessing preferred events, support personnel must know what constitutes those preferences. Second, it has also become well recognized that the traditional means of relying on opinions of teachers for identifying preferences among people with severe disabilities often does not result in accurate determinations of what these individuals truly like.

Research has consistently shown that teachers who work with learners with severe disabilities usually can identify learner preferences only under certain conditions. Unless those conditions are met, teacher opinion of what respective learners like usually will not correspond very accurately to the true likes of the learners. Specific steps must be taken to ensure teachers accurately identify learner preferences to incorporate within the teaching process as a means of enhancing learner enjoyment.

Steps that teachers can take to identify learner preferences vary along a continuum of practicality. Some ways are easily accomplished with little time and effort whereas other ways require rather considerable time and effort. The following sections describe the most common ways to identify preferences among learners who have severe disabilities. The most practical and easiest ways are presented first, followed by the more involved methods.

Relying on Teacher Opinion to Identify Learner Preferences

An individual's preferences range from what is most preferred in a given situation to what is least preferred. To illustrate, a learner may enjoy listening to music. Hence, listening to music represents a preferred activity for the learner. However, the learner may really like listening to hard rock, and also like listening to rap music but not as much as listening to hard rock. The learner may likewise enjoy listening to country music but not as much as listening to rap or hard rock. In regard to music listening as a preferred event for the learner, listening to hard rock is likely to be a strong preference, listening to rap a moderate preference, and listening to country a weak preference.

To enhance learner enjoyment with a teaching session, it is important to identify strong or at least moderate preferences (if something that is strongly preferred is not readily available to provide during a teaching session). The stronger the preference, the more likely that providing access to the preferred item or activity in conjunction with a teaching session will increase the learner's enjoyment.

There is a solid research base documenting that teachers are often accurate in identifying a respective learner's strongest preferences but are not very accurate in identifying moderate and weak preferences. Consequently, teachers may initially rely on their opinions to determine the most preferred items or activities to incorporate within the teaching process, but not rely solely on their opinions to determine other, less preferred items or activities. However, even relying on teacher opinion to identify the strongest preference or two for a learner will not be consistently accurate unless several conditions are met.

> **Opinions of support personnel typically reflect the strongest preferences of learners with severe disabilities more accurately than they reflect moderate and relatively weak preferences.**

The first condition necessary for a teacher's opinion to represent an accurate representation of a learner's strongest preferences is that the teacher must be very familiar with the learner. The teacher must have interacted repeatedly with the learner to become knowledgeable about the learner's usual activity patterns and methods of communication. If the pre-requisite has been met of the teacher spending time to establish a good relationship with the learner prior to beginning an instructional program, then usually the teacher will meet this condition.

The second condition that must be met is that the teacher must have spent time with the learner in the type of situation in which the teaching session will occur. If teaching will take place in a learner's group home, then the teacher must have spent time interacting with the learner in the group home. If teaching will take place in a classroom, then the teacher must have spent time with the learner during various classroom activities. This condition is necessary for the teacher to become familiar with the learner's activity patterns and communication mannerisms that may be idiosyncratic to a particular environment or situation.

It also can be most helpful if the teacher solicits the opinions of other personnel who are familiar with a given learner when attempting to identify preferred items and activities to incorporate within the teaching process. Generally, if three or four people all agree regarding what item or activity a learner likes the most within the situation in which teaching will occur, their joint opinion has a good likelihood of truly representing the learner's strongest preference.

A general rule of thumb is that if all of the conditions just summarized are met, then the teacher's opinion of a learner's most preferred items or activities can be incorporated within the teaching session to enhance learner enjoyment. If one or more of the conditions are not met, or if the teacher feels unsure about a learner's most preferred items or activities, then more specific steps should be taken to accurately identify the learner's preferences. Additionally, in order to accurately identify several different items or activities to incorporate within the teaching process beyond the most preferred item or activity, other steps must be taken by the teacher.

A teacher's opinion about a learner's most preferred items and activities is most likely to be accurate if:

1) the teacher is very familiar with the learner

2) the teacher has interacted frequently with the learner in the situation in which teaching will occur

3) the teacher's opinion about most preferred items and activities coincides with the opinion of other people who know the learner well

---

Informal Assessment Strategies for Identifying Learner Preferences

There are two relatively informal means that teachers can use to identify preferences among learners with severe disabilities beyond relying on personal opinion. Although the approaches may not result in totally accurate identification of all relative preferences, the strategies are usually helpful for determining several preferred items or activities to use within the teaching process. These methods involve *free access observations* and *repeated choices*.

Using free access observations to identify preferences. Free access situations involve a learner having access to several items or activities and being able to freely choose one with which to engage. The item or activity with which the learner engages the most usually represents the learner's strongest preference relative to all items and activities present. Hence, a teacher can arrange for several items or activities to be available for a learner and observe how much time the learner engages with each item or activity. Usually such a process must be performed on three to five different occasions for a teacher to obtain a clear picture of the learner's preferences. The following illustration demonstrates using this approach to identifying preferences.

Example of Using Free Access Observations
To Identify Preferences

A teacher has observed a learner with severe disabilities in a middle school classroom interact with several materials during leisure time in the afternoon, including a hand-held computer game, a picture book of classic automobiles, and drawing pad. However, the teacher does not know which of the three items the learner likes the most. In order to plan teaching sessions on a new learning objective for teaching the learner how to print his name, the teacher wants to know which of the three items is most preferred by the learner in order to provide the item immediately after conducting a name-writing teaching session. The teacher escorts the learner to a blocked off area of the classroom and presents each of the three items on a table. The teacher then observes how much time the learner engages with the computer game, the picture book, and the drawing pad after informing the learner that he can do what he wants in that area of the room for the next classroom period. This process is then repeated two more times across the next two school days. The teacher reviews her observation notes and finds that the learner spent more time looking at the picture book than playing the computer game and drawing on the pad. The teacher then decides to use the picture book as the most preferred item to provide after each teaching session is completed.

The free access process just described can be used with any learner who has the physical capability of approaching different items (or activities that the items represent). For ambulatory learners, items can simply be placed in a part of a room or on a table. For learners in wheelchairs, several items can be placed on the learners' wheelchair tray tops or on a table which is accessible to wheelchairs.

Sometimes when using the free access observation method to identify preferences, a learner will engage with only one of the available items or activities. When this happens, it is readily apparent what represents the learner's most preferred item or activity relative to all items and activities present. However, what will not be apparent in this situation is which of the other items or activities are more and less preferred relative to each other.

If a teacher desires to know several items or activities that may be relatively preferred in order to provide different items or activities during a teaching session, the teacher can remove the item or activity that is engaged with the most after several free access observations. In this manner, the latter item or activity is no longer available during the subsequent observation sessions, and the learner usually will engage most frequently with the next most preferred item or activity that is still available.

Using Repeated Choices to Identify Preferences. The second means of identifying learner preferences that can be conducted on a relatively informal basis involves providing a learner with repeated choices of two items or activities and observing which item or activity is chosen more frequently. In this process, three or four items or activities that a teacher believes may be of interest to a learner are initially selected. The teacher then presents two items or activities to the learner with an instruction to choose one of the items or activities. The learner is then given the opportunity to engage with the chosen item or activity for a few minutes. This process is then repeated later in the day and across different days, involving each item or activity being paired with every other item or activity for a choice presentation on at least three different occasions.

Using the process just described, the teacher can determine how often each item or activity is chosen most frequently when presented with all other items and activities, which item or activity is chosen the second most frequently, the third most frequently, etc. The item or activity chosen most frequently will typically represent the most preferred item or activity relative to all other items and activities that were involved in the choice presentations. Correspondingly, the item or activity chosen the second most frequently will represent the second strongest preference. In this manner, the teacher can identify a ranking of preferences across all items and activities.

> **Example of Using Repeated Choices To Identify Preferences**
>
> In the same example presented earlier in which a teacher wanted to determine which of three things a learner did during leisure time was most preferred, a repeated choice process could be used. The teacher could first ask the learner to choose between the computer game and the picture book, and then allow the learner to engage with the chosen item. Later that day, the teacher could then present the computer game and the drawing pad for the learner to choose one of the items with which to engage for a few minutes. Still later that day, the teacher could present the picture book and the drawing pad as a choice for the learner. These three choice presentations could be repeated across three or more days. Next, the teacher would determine the percentage of choice opportunities in which each of the three items was chosen. The item chosen the largest percentage of choice opportunities would represent the most preferred item, followed in turn by the item chosen the second largest percentage of opportunities and then by the item chosen on the smallest percentage of choice opportunities.

Formal Assessment Strategies for Identifying Preferences

For some learners, the informal means of identifying preferences as just described will not result in clear identification of specific preferences. Some learners may not engage with or choose any of the items or activities presented. Other learners may respond in highly inconsistent ways. If a teacher's informal attempts to identify preferences of a given learner do not prove successful, then more formal preference assessments can be conducted.

Formal means of identifying item and activity preferences of learners with severe disabilities are generally referred to as *systematic preference assessments*. A variety of systematic preference assessment procedures have been developed through applied research, and have proven quite reliable for identifying specific likes and dislikes of various learners. Most of the systematic preference assessments involve steps similar to those just described with the informal means of identifying preferences. However, the formal, systematic preference assessments involve more structured and precise procedures.

Because of the rather involved and technical nature of systematic preference assessments, they will not be described here. There are many other sources though that provide in-depth descriptions of how to conduct these types of preference assessments. The section on **Systematic Preference Assessments** in the **Selected Readings** later in this text presents what we have found to be among the most helpful descriptions of how to conduct systematic preference assessments.

Ensuring Preferred Items And Activities Are Presented As Part Of The Teaching Process

Regardless of how learner preferences are identified, those preferences must be incorporated within the teaching process. The main reason for exerting time and effort to accurately determine a respective learner's preferred items and activities is to be able to use them to enhance the learner's enjoyment with the teaching process. Once identified, the desired items and activities can be used within the teaching process through the *Preferred ABC Model* described previously. Using the *Model*, a teacher can decide whether to provide items and activities the learner likes as an antecedent to the teaching session, during the teaching session, and/or as a consequence to the session.

Chapter Review Questions

1. *What is the definitional relationship between a positive reinforcer and a preferred event?*

2. *What is an advantage of providing a preferred item or activity relative to providing a choice of items or activities as part of the teaching process?*

3. *What has research shown regarding the accuracy of relying on teacher opinion to identify preferred items and activities of learners?*

4. *What are three conditions that increase the accuracy of teacher opinion regarding preferred items and activities of learners?*

5. *How can preferences be identified using a free access method?*

6. *How can choices be used to identify preferences?*

7. *In what components of the Preferred ABC Model can preferred items and activities be used to enhance learner enjoyment with the teaching process?*

Chapter 9

The Timing Of Teaching: Considerations For When To Conduct Teaching Sessions

A primary consideration in planning a teaching session is *when* the session will be carried out with the learner. Several factors usually warrant attention in determining when to conduct a session. Practical issues often must be considered, such as when a teacher can arrange to have uninterrupted time with the learner to direct full attention to the teaching. The type of skill being taught also warrants attention in that some skills are best taught at times when the skills are naturally needed, whereas other skills can be taught at essentially any convenient time.

Among the various considerations in determining when to conduct a teaching session is one factor that can be critical for enhancing learner enjoyment: the *timing* of a teaching session. Timing pertains to when a teaching session is conducted relative to other ongoing activities in a learner's immediate environment. There are some situations in which the initiation of a teaching session is likely to be well received by a learner, with a corresponding likelihood that the learner will enjoy the session. There are other situations in which initiation of a teaching session will probably be poorly received by a learner, making it likely the learner will not enjoy the session. This chapter presents guidelines regarding times that are most and least advantageous to conduct teaching sessions in regard to learner enjoyment with the sessions.

> **A primary factor affecting a learner's enjoyment with a teaching session is the timing of when the session is initiated.**

Before presenting guidelines concerning the timing of teaching sessions, a caution warrants mention. Determining whether to conduct a teaching session with a learner at a given time often is guided more by subjective opinion than by evidence-based practices. Evidence-based practices for providing effective and enjoyable teaching sessions were discussed in **Chapter 2**. The primary point in addressing evidence-based practices was that instructional programs are more likely to teach skills to learners with disabilities in ways the learners enjoy if the programs have a scientific evidence base to substantiate their efficacy.

The significance of relying on evidence-based practices is particularly relevant when considering the timing of teaching sessions. As just indicated, decisions regarding when and when not to conduct a teaching session with a given learner frequently are made without regard for sound evidence to support the decisions. The following case example illustrates how reliance on factors other than empirical evidence for deciding whether to conduct a teaching session can be detrimental.

CASE EXAMPLE

Ms. Watson, a woman with profound cognitive and physical disabilities, resided in a congregate living situation and received adult education services in her residence. One of the educational/vocational goals for Ms. Watson was to teach her to cut paper with an adapted paper cutter. A direct support person was scheduled to carry out Ms. Watson's teaching program on a daily basis. When the staff person approached Ms. Watson to begin her teaching program, Ms. Watson frequently appeared nonalert, with her head down while sitting in her wheelchair and her eyes partially closed. Consequently, the staff person usually refrained from initiating Ms. Watson's program due to her apparent lack of alertness. The staff person's supervisor then recommended that the staff person attempt a few of the teaching trials with Ms. Watson even if she appeared nonalert. The supervisor suggested that if Ms. Watson's alertness did not improve after one or two teaching trials, then it would appear she was not sufficiently alert to benefit from the program. The supervisor also suggested that the initial teaching trials may actually help Ms. Watson become alert, such that

the remainder of the teaching session could then be carried out to her benefit. Following the supervisor's suggestion, the staff person found that when she began the teaching session even though Ms. Watson initially appeared nonalert, Ms. Watson's alertness quickly improved and she became responsive to the teaching trials.

In the example just illustrated, the teacher refrained from carrying out teaching sessions because the learner appeared nonalert and the teacher believed the learner would not benefit from instructional trials at those times. However, it became apparent that the learner's nonalertness was due to a lack of stimulation in her surrounding environment. When the teacher approached the learner to begin a teaching session, the learner had been sitting in her wheelchair without any ongoing activity for some time. The inactivity and lack of stimulation resulted in the learner becoming sleepy. When the teacher began the teaching session, the teacher's interactions with the learner as part of presenting instructional trials provided a type of social stimulation for the learner. Consequently, the learner quickly became alert once the teaching session was initiated.

The case example illustrates a situation that is relatively common in a number of agencies providing supports for people with highly significant disabilities. Teaching sessions are cancelled due to perceptions that individual learners are sleepy or otherwise nonalert. The lack of alertness though is often more a function of a nonstimulating environment than an internal condition on the part of the learners. By changing the social environment – in this case by initiating a teaching session – learners frequently can become much more alert.

Additional information regarding apparent alertness levels of learners with disabilities and whether a teaching session should be conducted will be provided later in this chapter. The point of concern here is that decisions regarding when to conduct and not conduct teaching sessions should be based on empirical evidence whenever possible. When a decision is made to withhold a teaching session, the decision should be based on evidence that indicates conducting a teaching session in the existing situation will be counterproductive to the learner's enjoyment or learning process.

Emphasizing that teaching sessions should not be withheld without evidence to indicate the sessions are not likely to be effective or enjoyable is necessary to avoid needless cancellation of teaching services. In some agencies, certain support personnel tend to find frequent reasons to avoid carrying out teaching programs. Although seemingly reasonable explanations are usually offered to justify the cancellations, the real reasons often pertain more to staff desire to avoid the time and effort required to conduct teaching sessions than to the learner's actual responsiveness to the teaching.

> **As a general rule, a teaching session should not be cancelled unless there is empirical evidence documenting that conducting the session in that situation will interfere with the learner's responsiveness or enjoyment.**

The situation just described should not be generalized to all situations in which teachers decide to cancel teaching sessions. In many cases, teachers honestly believe that a learner would not benefit at that point in time from a scheduled teaching session. Nonetheless, without empirical evidence to substantiate that a learner does not benefit from a teaching session under certain situations, teaching sessions may be needlessly cancelled. In turn, learners will be deprived of important instructional services.

The guidelines to be presented in the remainder of this chapter are based on behavior analytic research that identified situations affecting the likelihood of teaching sessions being effective and well received, or being ineffective and poorly received. In considering the guidelines, it is important to keep in mind that guidelines are meant to be flexible; they represent guides to follow in contrast to hard and fast rules.

Guidelines for The Timing of Teaching Sessions

In considering guidelines for the timing of teaching sessions, the other means of enhancing learner enjoyment with teaching sessions should not be forgotten. In many ways, the guidelines to be presented will be more effective if the previously discussed ways of enhancing learner enjoyment are already in place. It should also be noted that the following guidelines are not mutually exclusive. All of the guidelines should be considered by a teacher when deciding the best time to conduct a teaching session.

Guideline 1: Avoid Interrupting an Ongoing, Highly Preferred Activity of A Learner to Conduct a Teaching Session

This guideline pertains to when a teaching session should not be conducted. If a learner is actively engaged in a highly preferred activity when a teaching session is scheduled to occur, the session should be postponed if at all possible. If a teacher interrupts a learner's ongoing activity which the learner is clearly enjoying, the learner is likely to become discontented with the teacher and subsequent participation in the teaching session. Such discontent can decrease the learner's enjoyment with the teaching session. The discontent also can set the occasion for serious problem behavior by the learner. Problem behavior, such as aggressing toward the teacher, may occur as a means for the learner to attempt to stop the teacher from discontinuing the ongoing activity. Problem behavior will be used to get the teacher to leave the learner alone.

In considering a learner's involvement in a highly preferred activity as a reason to temporarily postpone a teaching session, it should be clarified that the focus here is on an activity that is already ongoing prior to the initiation of a teaching session. As discussed in preceding chapters, teaching sessions themselves should begin with a brief presentation of a preferred activity or item. In the latter case, the preferred item or activity is actually part of the overall teaching process. The concern here is when a learner is involved in a preferred activity *before* any aspect of the teaching process is initiated, such that the already ongoing preferred activity would have to be terminated in order to begin the teaching process.

The most proactive approach to avoiding discontent and problem behavior due to a learner not wanting to stop an ongoing activity to participate in a teaching session is to avoid scheduling a session during or immediately following a learner's highly preferred activity. Teachers should consider the daily schedule and where possible, plan teaching sessions for those periods that do not follow a typically scheduled, highly preferred activity by the learner. For example, a teacher could consider conducting a formal teaching session following a transition time such as after coming back to a school classroom after having been to the restroom. Transition times usually do not represent highly preferred activities, such that following these situations with teaching sessions are not likely to occasion discontent and problem behavior.

Another time that can be opportune to initiate teaching sessions for some learners is after the learners finish working on tasks that they know how to do but are expected to perform for practice purposes. These types of activities, such as practicing writing alphabet letters or completing previously learned vocational tasks, often require little teacher interaction with the learner. The learner knows how to perform the tasks and likely requires minimal help from the teacher to complete the tasks. In contrast, teaching sessions involve repeated interactions with the teacher. The latter interactions involve increased attention from the teacher relative to the amount of teacher attention provided to the learner during the former activities. If the teacher has established a good relationship with the learner as stressed repeatedly throughout this text, initiation of the teaching session is likely to be well received by the learner because it signals desired attention from the teacher.

> **Teaching sessions in which a teacher repeatedly provides positive attention to a learner are likely to be more enjoyable if the sessions follow periods of time in which the learner received minimal or no attention from the teacher.**

Sometimes a teacher cannot realistically postpone a teaching session even though a learner is observed to be actively engaged in an enjoyable activity. It may be the end of the teacher's day with the learner and there is no time to postpone teaching for that day, or another activity may be forthcoming that would prohibit postponing the teaching session. In these situations, it can be helpful if the teacher informs the learner that the teaching session will begin in a few minutes or other specified period of time. Such a *signal* that the ongoing activity will need to be halted and a teaching session initiated can help the learner adapt to the forthcoming change. Some learners respond more favorably to a subsequent change in activity if they are clearly aware of the change beforehand relative to changes that occur abruptly without preceding awareness.

Similar to signaling that an ongoing activity will soon stop and a teaching session will occur is giving the learner a choice of participating in a teaching session. In this case the choice involves taking part in the teaching session at that moment or waiting to begin the session later as described in **Chapter 7**. As also discussed in **Chapter 7**, this type of choice is not always practical to provide. When it can be provided though, the choice opportunity has the advantages discussed previously in terms of giving the learner some control over the teaching session. The choice presentation also serves in essence as a signal that a teaching session is forthcoming (if the learner chooses to postpone the teaching session for a little while).

To increase learner enjoyment and prevent possible discontent when a teaching session is initiated, a teacher can:

1) avoid interrupting a highly preferred, ongoing activity whenever possible or,

2) if avoiding interruption of a highly preferred, ongoing activity is not possible, inform the learner of the forthcoming teaching session prior to beginning the session

---

Guideline 2: Use Preferred Events in Teaching Sessions That The Learner has Limited Access to Before the Sessions

The importance of providing preferred items and activities before, during, and after a teaching session to enhance learner enjoyment has been discussed in previous chapters. Essentially, the more preferred the events incorporated within the teaching process, the more the learner will enjoy the teaching session.

One means of increasing the likelihood that preferred events used in teaching sessions will be truly enjoyed by the learner is to conduct sessions following times when the learner has limited access to the preferred items and activities. When a learner goes for a period of time without experiencing preferred events, then the preferred nature of those items and activities is heightened when presented as part of the teaching process. In contrast, if a learner frequently engages with the preferred items and activities prior to a teaching session, then their preferred nature will be diminished when presented during the teaching process.

Correspondingly, the effect of the preferred events on learner enjoyment with teaching is enhanced in the former situations and reduced in the latter.

The effect of conducting a teaching session following periods in which a learner has varying degrees of access to preferred events that are used in teaching is most apparent with food and drink items. To illustrate, if a learner likes drinking a diet soda and consumes a diet soda right before a teaching session is initiated, the learner is not likely to want a soda very much when it is provided as part of the teaching process. Providing the soda will do little to enhance the learner's enjoyment with the teaching session. On the other hand, if a teaching session occurs in early afternoon and the learner has not had a diet soda during the day, then the learner will probably like drinking the soda when it is provided during the teaching process. Having access to the soda as part of the teaching session will help the learner enjoy participating in the session.

The same type of effect just summarized also exists with preferred events other than consuming food and drink items. The situation noted earlier in which teacher attention provided during a teaching session is more likely to be highly preferred if the session follows a period of time in which the learner received little attention represents another example. In the latter situation, the learner has limited access to teacher attention during an ongoing activity, which heightens the preferred nature of the attention when it is provided during a subsequent teaching session.

Essentially, the less frequently a learner experiences a preferred event during the day, the more enjoyment the learner will experience when that event eventually does occur. If the event is part of the teaching process, then the teaching tends to be associated by the learner with something highly preferred. Such an association increases a learner's enjoyment with the overall teaching situation.

To capitalize on the increased desirability of preferred events that occurs when access to the events is limited, a teacher must plan the timing of a teaching session carefully. Thinking through the typical schedule of daily activities can usually reveal time periods during which a learner is not likely to have had access to certain preferred events. It can be advantageous to schedule teaching sessions that involve those particular events after the identified time periods.

CASE EXAMPLE

Seth, a kindergartner with autism, really liked going out to play during recess. Recess was regularly scheduled as part of the classroom routine to occur in the early afternoon. One of the teaching programs which appeared to be disliked by Seth involved teaching him how to print. He often resisted teacher attempts to prompt him to print letters and often whined and otherwise vocalized his displeasure. The teacher began scheduling the letter-printing session during the half-hour period prior to when recess was scheduled. Going to recess was the highly preferred activity that the teacher then provided immediately upon Seth's completion of the assigned letter-printing task. After Seth experienced being able to go outside to play immediately after finishing the printing, his negative vocalizations and resistance decreased, and he completed the task more readily.

In the example just illustrated, the learner had no access to the activity of going to recess during the day except in the afternoon. Hence, when the opportunity arose later in the day to go outside to play, it represented a strong preference for the learner. By scheduling the teaching session such that it was immediately followed by the opportunity to go outside and play, the teaching session started to function as the beginning of a highly preferred event for the learner.

When considering limitations in access to preferred events, it should be noted that the intent is not to deprive a learner from basic necessities or naturally occurring preferred events. Rather, the intent is to schedule teaching sessions that involve various preferred events following time periods in which those events are not normally available to the learner. Carefully scheduling the timing of teaching sessions in this manner can increase the likelihood that events incorporated into the teaching process will be highly preferred by the learner and enhance the learner's enjoyment with the teaching.

Guideline 3: Consider Building Consistency Into the Timing of Teaching Sessions

For some learners, and especially individuals with particular types of disabilities such as autism and Asperger's Syndrome, consistency and predictability of the daily routine is very important. These individuals appear to prefer following a predictable schedule with daily events. When there is a change in the usual schedule, such as when an unanticipated event occurs, they can experience significant discontent.

In some cases, individuals will engage in serious problem behavior such as a tantrum or self-injury following an unanticipated change in the schedule. The problem behavior often occurs as a means for the learner to attempt to avoid participating in the unpredicted event, or to bring predictability back into the schedule. For example, a learner may engage in self-injurious head hitting following the presentation of an unanticipated activity by a teacher in an attempt to get the teacher to implement part of the learner's behavior support plan. The learner knows what the teacher will do following a self-injurious episode, due to previous self-injurious episodes which were followed by the teacher implementing the support plan. Implementation of the plan represents a degree of predictability for the learner relative to initiation of the unanticipated event.

For learners who prefer a set schedule, it can be advantageous to follow a consistent routine in terms of when teaching sessions occur. Maintaining a predictable schedule of teaching sessions for these learners can reduce discontent and prevent problem behavior that can occur if the teaching schedule is not consistent.

Many teachers are well aware that certain learners perform better when their daily schedule is highly consistent. These teachers are also aware though that sometimes teaching sessions cannot always occur on a consistent basis. In these cases, learner discontent with an unanticipated teaching session often can be reduced by signaling to the learner about a forthcoming teaching session (see similar discussion concerning **Guideline 1** on using signals to avoid problems with interruption of highly preferred activities).

For learners who appear to prefer consistency with their daily routine, attempts should be made to conduct teaching sessions on a consistent and predictable schedule.

Guideline 4: Consider Apparent State Condition When Planning to Initiate a Teaching Session

Probably the most difficult timing decision facing teachers when planning to initiate a teaching session is when a learner appears to be experiencing what is considered an unusual *state condition.* An unusual state condition refers to a learner appearing to act much differently than normal without an immediately apparent explanation for the behavior. To illustrate, a learner may appear to be very upset or angry at a time when nothing noticeable occurred in the learner's immediate environment that would be expected to upset the learner. Similarly, a learner may be much more agitated than usual, or much less responsive to usual social interactions.

When situations arise such as those just exemplified, they are sometimes referred to as unusual state conditions because it is presumed that the atypical activity pattern is due to the biological state of the person. It may be assumed, for example, the learner is having a bad reaction to a change in medication, or may be having increased seizure activity. At other times it is assumed that the learner may be experiencing physical discomfort (e.g., due to allergies or a headache) and typical medical symptoms of the discomfort have not yet become apparent.

Determining whether to proceed with a planned teaching session when a learner appears to be experiencing an unusual state condition is difficult. The learner's biological status, such as feeling ill, may interfere with the ability to respond appropriately to instructional trials. In other cases, the learner may be able to respond appropriately with increased effort to instructional trials, but the process may be unpleasant for the learner. The learner's enjoyment with a teaching session in such situations can be seriously jeopardized. In still other cases, such as the example presented earlier involving a learner who appeared nonalert, conducting the teaching session can help the learner overcome the existing state condition. Hence, when a learner appears to be experiencing what may be considered an unusual state condition, the teacher can be faced with a difficult decision of whether conducting the teaching session at that time would be beneficial or detrimental for the learner.

Before summarizing recommendations for making decisions about conducting teaching sessions with a learner who appears to be in an unusual state condition, a point of caution is warranted. Many people in the human services frequently attribute unusual behavior of an individual with a significant disability to some type of internal state condition. While state conditions do exist that can affect unusual behavior patterns, they represent only one of many possible causes. In a large number of situations, upon close scrutiny certain environmental changes can be identified that tend to coincide with -- and likely occasion -- unusual behavior patterns. Even when environmental changes are not immediately detected, doing something with the learner such as conducting a teaching session can help the learner overcome the existing state condition as referred to earlier. In short, withholding teaching services because unusual behavior patterns are attributed to an individual's internal state must be done cautiously.

When a learner demonstrates unusual behavior patterns and no environmental changes can be identified that may account for the patterns, teachers must be systematic in how they determine whether to cancel a scheduled teaching session. Needlessly canceling a teaching session can deprive a learner of important services, whereas proceeding with a session when the learner is likely to have difficulty responding or enjoying the session can be unfair as well as unpleasant for the learner.

Being systematic means that a teacher takes an evidence-based approach in deciding whether to proceed with a teaching session. In this case, evidence-based does not refer to basing a decision on results of scientific research. Such information would not be readily available in many situations for dealing with unusual behavior patterns of an unknown cause. Rather, evidence-based in this situation means the teacher progresses through several systematic steps. The teacher then carefully judges a learner's response to the steps before deciding whether to proceed with the teaching session.

The steps a teacher should take involve initiating a teaching session and carefully observing the learner's immediate response. If the learner clearly shows less response to instructional trials than usual, or shows less enjoyment with the teaching process, then the teacher is well justified in discontinuing the teaching session at that point. However, such a decision should not be permanent. The teacher should repeat the process on several occasions in order to obtain a more complete picture of how the learner responds when an unusual state condition seems to exist.

It is also helpful if a teacher maintains records of the learner's responses when teaching sessions are discontinued due to an apparent state condition. Records of those responses should then be compared to when the learner is responding more typically. These comparison data provide the evidence base to support a decision to cancel a teaching session when an apparent state condition exists if the data show a clear difference in responding in the two situations. Until such an evidence base exists, a teacher should usually proceed with a teaching session even if an apparent state condition seems to exist, and then discontinue the session only when unusual responding is observed during the teaching.

> **Deciding to cancel a teaching session due to an apparent state condition of a learner should be done cautiously and with an evidence base to support the decision.**

It warrants re-iteration that the just noted recommendations represent only guidelines. There will likely be times, for example, when it is very clear that a learner is experiencing a particular state condition that dictates cancellation of a teaching session, such as when a learner is extremely tired after having an observed seizure. There are no well-established guidelines based on scientific evidence for these types of conditions; the teacher must rely on basic common sense. If various state conditions appear to occur repeatedly for a given learner, the teacher should convene the learner's support team together or other group of relevant personnel to carefully review the situation and determine the most beneficial course of action.

> **Guidelines for Considering When to Conduct a Teaching Session**
>
> Avoid interrupting an ongoing, highly preferred activity
>
> Conduct a session after a period in which a learner has had limited access to preferred items and activities to be used in the session
>
> Consider consistency of when teaching sessions are scheduled
>
> Consider conducting a session when a learner appears in an unusual state condition based on data regarding likely response in that condition

Chapter Review Questions

1. *What detrimental outcome is likely to occur if decisions to conduct or not conduct a teaching session are made without a strong evidence base?*

2. *What is one situation based on an ongoing environmental activity in which it is generally not advised to begin a teaching session?*

3. *For learners who tend not to like unexpected changes in the daily routine, what can be done before a change occurs that is likely to reduce their discontent with the change?*

4. *Describe how access to certain preferred events should affect when a teaching session is conducted.*

5. *What is meant by an apparent state condition, and how should decisions be made about conducting teaching sessions or not when such a condition appears to exist?*

Section IV

Keeping Teaching Enjoyable

Chapter 10

Enhancing Teacher Enjoyment

In the introductory comments to this text, the importance of teachers enjoying the teaching process was noted. It was emphasized that when teachers do not enjoy carrying out teaching programs, learner enjoyment with the programs is almost always compromised. In essence, the less a teacher enjoys carrying out teaching programs, the less likely it is that learners will enjoy participating in the programs.

Lack of teacher enjoyment in conducting teaching programs also affects learner skill acquisition. When teachers do not enjoy teaching, there is a tendency to hurry through teaching programs or to conduct programs in an incomplete manner. There is also a tendency to avoid carrying out some teaching programs altogether. The end result is that teaching programs are not carried out as designed, and their effectiveness for promoting learner skill acquisition is diminished.

Failure to conduct teaching programs in the appropriate manner represents unprofessional and generally unacceptable performance among personnel charged with teaching responsibilities. Teaching programs must be carried out appropriately if learners with disabilities are to receive services they are intended to receive, and to have opportunities to learn meaningful skills.

> **Lack of teacher enjoyment in conducting teaching sessions often reduces learner enjoyment and the effectiveness of the teaching.**

The amount of enjoyment a teacher experiences with the teaching process also has important implications for the teacher. Most apparently, if a teacher does not enjoy carrying out teaching programs, the teacher's quality of work life will be affected. Quality of work life is directly related to an individual's degree of enjoyment with daily work activities. When a teacher routinely performs certain duties that are not enjoyable, such as carrying out teaching programs, overall enjoyment with the job will be reduced significantly.

To promote and maintain enjoyment with the teaching process, teachers should take active steps. Teaching learners with developmental disabilities can be an effortful and demanding responsibility. It should not be assumed that carrying out teaching programs with every learner will be naturally enjoyable. This chapter describes steps teachers can take to enhance their enjoyment in fulfilling teaching responsibilities. Four ways to promote enjoyment with teaching are presented:

- **Increase learner enjoyment with teaching programs**

- **Use naturalistic teaching**

- **Self-motivational steps**

- **Recruit support from others**

Increase Learner Enjoyment With Teaching Programs

Just as lack of teacher enjoyment with a teaching program will reduce how much a learner likes a program, a learner's dislike of a teaching program will detract from the teacher's enjoyment. Conversely, if a learner clearly enjoys participating in a teaching program, that enjoyment will usually help the teacher enjoy the teaching process. Hence, one means of helping teachers enjoy teaching programs is to ensure their learners enjoy participating in the programs.

Procedures discussed in preceding chapters for helping individuals with developmental disabilities enjoy learning have a strong evidence base to support their efficacy. By including the procedures within the teaching process, teachers are very likely to enhance learner enjoyment with teaching programs. A secondary yet important outcome of using the procedures is that teacher enjoyment is also enhanced.

Promoting learner enjoyment with teaching programs increases teacher enjoyment with the programs in several ways. One major way is that when a learner enjoys participating in teaching programs, the learner is not likely to display problem behavior. Problem behavior during a teaching session usually occurs because a learner does not want to participate in the session or does not like some aspect of the teaching process. Learners will complain, aggress, destroy property, and even engage in self-injury in attempts to avoid or escape participating in teaching sessions they do not like. If teaching programs are enjoyable for learners, there will be no reason for the learners to engage in problem behavior to avoid or escape the programs.

Dealing with problem behavior is typically most unpleasant for teachers. Repeatedly being hit, bit, or spit at, for example, is clearly not enjoyable. When teachers are faced with these types of problem behaviors during teaching sessions, there is little enjoyment in conducting the sessions. Eliminating problem behavior by making teaching programs enjoyable prevents teachers from experiencing such behavior.

Another way learner enjoyment with teaching programs enhances teacher enjoyment is that it can be inherently pleasing for teachers to witness their learners enjoying themselves. It is hard for teachers not to be pleased when they observe that individuals with disabilities are enjoying working with the teachers on instructional programs.

> **Enhancing learner enjoyment with teaching programs reduces the likelihood of problem behavior, and makes the teaching process inherently more enjoyable for the teacher**.

Supplement Teaching Programs With Naturalistic Teaching

Our discussion throughout this text has focused on formal teaching programs. Procedures for making teaching enjoyable have been discussed regarding situations in which teachers provide individualized learner attention for the explicit purpose of conducting a task-analyzed teaching program. Formal teaching programs are an integral part of the learning process for individuals with developmental disabilities.

Although formal programs conducted during circumscribed sessions represent a well-established means of teaching individuals with disabilities, there is another important way to provide instruction: *naturalistic teaching*. Naturalistic teaching refers to providing aspects of instruction during naturally occurring activities and routines for learners. This method of teaching is sometimes referred to as embedded teaching, because instructional trials are embedded within ongoing activities. Naturalistic teaching is also referred to as incidental teaching at times, because the teaching occurs somewhat incidentally as instructional opportunities arise during the daily routine.

Regardless of the particular descriptors used, all naturalistic teaching procedures are similar in that they are conducted as part of typically occurring activities for learners. In contrast to formal teaching sessions explicitly conducted for the sole purpose of carrying out instruction, naturalistic teaching occurs during ongoing activities that have other purposes for learners. For example, instructional trials may be embedded within meal or snack times, during regularly occurring recreational outings, or as part of ongoing work duties. The **Naturalistic Teaching** section in the **Selected Readings** provides references to detailed accounts of how naturalistic teaching procedures can be conducted as part of the routine day.

The reason for addressing naturalistic teaching here is that this instructional approach often represents an enjoyable event for learners. Naturalistic teaching procedures are frequently incorporated within preferred learner activities that occur during the normal course of the day. By being part of preferred activities, the teaching procedures themselves come to be preferred by learners.

Naturalistic teaching procedures are usually well received by learners for several reasons. Each reason pertains to how and when the procedures are used within various activities. For example, one common application of naturalistic teaching pertains to when a learner is naturally motivated to seek something, but requires assistance to obtain what is desired. In such a situation, a teacher can prompt the learner to use a newly acquired skill, or one that is currently being taught in formal teaching sessions, while assisting the learner in obtaining what is desired.

To illustrate, a learner may want a magazine that is in a cabinet but cannot open the cabinet. When the teacher observes the learner attempting to open the cabinet, the teacher can intervene and prompt the learner to communicate what is wanted using a communication means (saying, signing, etc.) that the teacher has been teaching the learner in formal sessions. Once the learner communicates, even if a least-to-most helpful prompt strategy is required from the teacher for assistance (**Chapter 3**), the teacher can then open the cabinet and provide the learner with the desired magazine.

In the situation just summarized, the learner is naturally motivated to seek the magazine. When the magazine is obtained following the learner's prompted communication, the learner is likely pleased to have received the desired object. Because the teacher's assistance through instructional prompting resulted in the learner obtaining something desired and is therefore pleasing to the learner, the teaching assistance is associated with something the learner enjoys. In this manner, the teaching process itself tends to become something the learner likes.

Another reason naturalistic teaching procedures are usually well received by learners is that the procedures are often applied in typical community environments with other people. Naturalistic teaching can occur in essentially any community environment such as grocery stores, parks, malls, and movie theaters. Learners with disabilities, just like everybody else, frequently enjoy participating in community situations in which there are other people to watch and interact with, as well as a variety of activities in which to participate. By incorporating brief instructional trials as part of the community activities, such as by prompting and reinforcing a greeting skill or object-naming skill for example, the instruction is associated with an enjoyable experience.

> **Naturalistic teaching is usually well received by learners and increases enjoyment for teachers.**

An opportune time to conduct naturalistic teaching is when a learner has mastered or almost mastered a skill being taught in formal teaching sessions. For instance, a teacher may be teaching an adolescent with severe cognitive disabilities how to purchase a soda from a vending machine in the school cafeteria. Following a number of formal teaching sessions with task-analyzed instructional trials in the cafeteria, the learner is successfully purchasing sodas. The teacher may then escort the learner to various community settings during the week to provide the student opportunities to use the newly acquired skills with different vending machines. Because some vending machines are different than others, the learner is likely to require some teacher assistance to operate certain machines. The teacher can use brief prompting and praise to help the learner purchase a soda from the different machines in a naturalistic teaching manner.

In the illustration just provided, the learner is likely to be pleased with using the newly learned skills in different locations. For one thing, the learner probably enjoys the sodas once purchased. The learner also is likely to feel good about successfully completing a desired task, representing a source of control and independence for the learner. Enjoyment the learner demonstrates in turn helps the teacher feel good about what has been accomplished.

Naturalistic teaching procedures should be used to supplement formal teaching programs both to enhance learner application of skills being acquired through the programs and learner enjoyment with the teaching process. Again, when a learner enjoys taking part in teaching activities, the teacher usually experiences enjoyment as well.

Self-Motivation For Teachers

Making teaching enjoyable for learners and naturalistic teaching represent ways to enhance teacher enjoyment due in part to the inherently rewarding aspects of teaching. Most teachers find it very satisfying when their learners acquire new skills as a function of the teachers' instructional efforts. Most teachers also experience significant pleasure when it is apparent that learners have enjoyed the teaching process.

Despite the important effect learner responsiveness to teaching programs can have on a teacher's enjoyment, teachers should not rely solely on this means of maintaining enjoyment with teaching. Teachers must take other steps to ensure they enjoy teaching duties on a day-to-day basis. Teaching learners with significant disabilities requires persistence, effort, and patience. If teachers do not actively strive to maintain enjoyment with the teaching process beyond benefits derived from observing individuals enjoy learning, their enjoyment will likely wane.

There are several key steps teachers can take to help themselves enjoy teaching learners with disabilities. Before describing these steps though, some discussion is warranted over the importance of actively attempting to motivate oneself to enjoy teaching. Many people discount the notion of being able to do things to motivate themselves. Motivation is viewed as an inherent trait, and some people are simply considered highly motivated and some are not.

There is certainly validity to the concept of inherent motivation. However, reliance on inherent motivation without actively promoting one's motivation is risky. Many things can happen in work settings in which teachers carry out teaching programs that are unpleasant or distasteful for teachers. When negative things happen frequently, whether due to actions by their supervisors, undesirable attributes of the physical work environment, or unpleasant activities involving co-workers, quality of work life among teachers can be seriously eroded. Even the most dedicated and motivated teachers can lose their enjoyment with teaching responsibilities if the work environment becomes consistently unpleasant. In these situations, it is paramount that teachers actively take steps to maintain their motivation and enjoyment with teaching.

In other situations, teaching personnel consider work motivation to be the responsibility of their supervisors. Supervisors should indeed actively strive to motivate staff who have teaching duties (see **Chapter 11** for discussion on what supervisors should do to support teachers). However, teachers should not be entirely dependent on their supervisors as a source of motivation. Some supervisors are not very concerned about motivating their staff. These supervisors may be overly focused on their own work agenda, or not willing to exert the effort required to provide a motivating work environment for staff. Other supervisors may want to motivate staff, but not know how to provide a motivating environment.

In short, teachers should not rely solely on others to help them enjoy their teaching responsibilities. Teachers should assume control of their own enjoyment with teaching and take active steps to achieve and maintain enjoyment. The following three steps have proven quite successful for helping people in the human services motivate themselves to work both effectively and enjoyably.

Self-motivation for teachers can be achieved by taking active steps to enhance their enjoyment with teaching.

Step 1: Develop Goals For Teaching Programs

The first step for helping oneself stay motivated and enjoy carrying out teaching programs is to establish short-term goals. The goals should relate to respective teaching programs and should be achievable within a few days, or at least within a week's period of time. Examples of common short-term goals related to conducting teaching programs include:

- **Carrying out a given program a criterion number of times during the week**

- **Conducting a program as many times as necessary over a five-day period until a learner demonstrates a certain level of progress**

- **Re-designing a program to include more procedures to enhance learner enjoyment by the end of the work day**

Establishing goals that can be achieved within a few days has several motivational benefits. First, by setting a clear goal relating to a teaching responsibility, a teacher's attention on fulfilling that responsibility is likely to become more focused. Second, awareness of having an explicit goal to achieve can make working toward that goal more enjoyable for a teacher. Once an explicit goal is set, a certain amount of enthusiasm is often generated in terms of completing teaching responsibilities in order to meet the goal.

It also can be helpful if the goal that a teacher establishes is written down. Once the goal is achieved, the teacher should then record in some manner that the goal has been met. Self-recording attainment of goals is another means of helping to generate enthusiasm for fulfilling teaching responsibilities.

Although there are motivational benefits derived from setting short-term goals inherent in the process itself, the most important benefit is more of a pre-requisite nature. Establishing goals sets the occasion for effectively completing the remaining steps in the self-motivational process.

Step 2: Achieve The Teaching Goals

Once a short-term goal is established regarding certain teaching responsibilities, the next step is to achieve the goal. Goals are of little use if they are not achieved. Self-motivation by definition means that one takes action to promote diligent and enjoyable work performance. Completing work duties necessary to achieve a designated goal represents the diligence part of self-motivation.

Step 3: Do Something Highly Preferred

The final step in the self-motivational approach to enhancing enjoyment with teaching is for teachers to do something highly preferred once they have achieved their established goal. In essence, teachers should positively reinforce their accomplishment by doing something they enjoy. Engaging in a highly preferred event following attainment of a goal can help teachers stay motivated to continue establishing and attaining teaching goals. Such a process also provides a source of enjoyment through participation in the preferred activity.

It is generally beneficial if teachers determine their preferred activity to engage in upon attaining a teaching goal when the goal is initially established (as part of Step 1). Knowing what will be done for enjoyment upon meeting the goal can increase interest in working toward the goal. Awareness of the forthcoming participation in something highly desired can also make the work more enjoyable.

What a teacher does for enjoyment after attaining a teaching goal depends on the interests and preferences of the teacher. The preferred activity can be something within the work place, provided of course that the activity complies with what is acceptable within the teacher's agency. For example, a teacher may engage in a desired leisure activity with one or more learners, or spend time on a special work project that is more enjoyable than typical work duties. Alternatively, a teacher may schedule a preferred activity outside of work as a means of recognizing and enjoying the accomplishment of attaining a desired outcome with a teaching program. We have worked with many colleagues who celebrate their short-term work accomplishments with enjoyable activities outside of work, ranging from treating themselves to a favorite dinner to going fishing.

Just as some persons disregard the concept of taking active steps to motivate themselves, many people believe that self-reinforcement activities as just exemplified have little utility. However, there is a substantial body or research demonstrating that the process of engaging in a preferred activity following one's accomplishments can promote continued work effort as well as enjoyment with work activities. By providing enjoyable activities for themselves following attainment of a self-established work goal, teachers are in essence taking control of their own motivation. Having control over motivation to work diligently and enjoyably reduces dependency on others for providing a desirable quality of work life.

> **The process of setting a teaching goal, achieving the goal, and engaging in a preferred activity to celebrate the achievement helps teachers take charge of their work motivation and overall quality of work life.**

Secure Support From Others

Similar to taking charge of one's motivation, a teacher can promote support from others for their teaching accomplishments. Although teachers should not be entirely dependent on others for motivation, securing support from other persons can be one part of the overall motivational process. Teachers should set the occasion for other people to support their teaching achievements.

Most of us like it when other people are aware of our successes. We also are usually pleased when others recognize what we have accomplished. Receiving such recognition can help make the time and effort invested in teaching more enjoyable for teachers.

Setting the occasion to receive support from other people with whom a teacher works or interacts does not require teachers to brag or otherwise engage in self-promoting activities. Setting the occasion for support simply means doing things during the routine course of the work day that helps other individuals be aware of teaching successes.

One of the best ways to set the occasion for support is to let others know when a learner has succeeded in learning an important skill. This is one of the indirect benefits of naturalistic teaching procedures conducted once a learner has demonstrated progress during formal teaching programs. Because naturalistic teaching occurs in typical community environments, other people are likely to witness a learner performing an important skill. Some people will then favorably acknowledge the learner's accomplishment to the learner or the teacher. Such praise can be quite pleasant for both the learner and the teacher, and represent a small but important source of enjoyment for the teacher.

Teachers can also let others know about a learner's success in learning new skills during routine interactions with other personnel in the agency and family members of the learner. Informing others about a learner's accomplishments is a professionally acceptable act for teachers, and teachers should not be hesitant to express approval about a learner's successes. Indeed, helping learners attain important outcomes, such as learning new skills, is one of the primary missions of agencies in which teaching services are provided. Teachers can comment on learner accomplishments in informal interactions with others in the work place as well as during regularly occurring staff meetings.

> **Publicly commending learner accomplishments can enhance learner and teacher enjoyment with teaching programs.**

An indirect but important means of setting the occasion for securing support from others for teaching accomplishments is to actively support the teaching achievements of other teachers. Such support is readily provided by praising other teachers for success in helping their learners acquire meaningful skills. Praising other teachers for teaching accomplishments is a nice way to help them enjoy their teaching responsibilities, which in turn can have long-term benefits for their continued teaching efforts with learners.

There are also benefits for a teacher who praises the teaching successes of co-workers. Such actions make it apparent that the teacher values good teaching, which can foster respect among co-workers. When a teacher praises the actions of others, the teacher also is modeling a type of positive support. Modeling positive support through praise can encourage other people to support and acknowledge teaching accomplishments. Consequently, other people are more likely to commend the teacher when they become aware of the teacher's own accomplishments with learners.

In addition to co-workers and family members of learners, teachers can set the occasion for receiving support from their supervisors. Teachers should make supervisors aware of learner accomplishments within the teaching process in basically the same ways they make their co-workers aware of the successes. Such awareness can foster supportive praise from supervisors in the same manner it promotes support from co-workers.

Many supervisors are especially pleased when their teaching staff approach them with information about desirable accomplishments of learners. Part of the pleasure supervisors experience in these situations occurs because many supervisors are accustomed to staff approaching them only when there are problems to report, or staff need something from the supervisors. When a staff person contacts a supervisor for the sole purpose of informing the supervisor something positive has been accomplished, the information is in contrast to the usual negative information that a supervisor commonly receives. Such contrast makes the positive aspects of the learner's accomplishments, as well as the teacher's successful performance, stand out noticeably for the supervisor.

Supervisors often become more likely to support those teachers who provide them with favorable information about learners in their agency. Good supervisors consistently look for accomplishments of learners and staff responsible for the successes to commend and otherwise support admirable staff performance. Elaboration on what supervisors can and should do to support teaching efforts of their staff is provided in the following chapter.

Chapter Review Questions

1. *How does learner enjoyment with teaching programs affect teacher enjoyment with the programs and vice versa?*

2. *What are four ways teachers can increase their enjoyment in carrying out teaching programs?*

3. *What is naturalistic teaching and how can it enhance learner enjoyment with teaching procedures?*

4. *What are three key steps for teacher self-motivation?*

5. *How can learner accomplishments be applied by teachers to secure support from others for the teachers?*

Chapter 11

Supervisory Responsibilities For Supporting Teaching Effectiveness And Enjoyment

The degree of success teachers have in making teaching programs enjoyable for learners with disabilities depends on several factors. A most apparent factor is the efficacy of procedures used to enhance learner enjoyment. Teacher skills and motivation for proficiently implementing programs are also apparent factors. Another factor that is not so apparent yet is critical to the long-term success of teachers is the quality of their work environment. The environment in which teachers work can significantly enhance or hinder their efforts to help individuals with disabilities enjoy learning.

Providing a work environment that promotes successful teaching performance is the explicit responsibility of agency supervisors. Agencies that consistently provide the highest quality teaching services are characterized by supervisors who work actively and effectively to support their teaching staff. If supervisors do not provide a supportive environment for teachers, helping individuals enjoy learning will be difficult for even the most skillful and dedicated teachers.

There are many aspects involved in providing a supportive work environment for teachers in human service agencies. Some aspects vary depending on the nature of the agency, such as a school versus a group home or vocational center. Specifically in regard to supporting teachers in helping people with disabilities enjoy learning, there are also some consistent features across all agencies. Agency supervisors must ensure those features are in place if teachers are to successfully fulfill teaching duties on a regular basis.

> **It is the explicit responsibility of agency supervisors to provide a work environment that supports teachers in fulfilling teaching duties in an effective and enjoyable manner.**

This chapter summarizes the most important aspects of what supervisors should do to support teachers in fulfilling their teaching responsibilities. The focus is on what supervisors can do on a day-to-day basis to provide a supportive and motivating work environment for teachers.

Espousing Agency Values That Support Learner Skill Acquisition And Enjoyment

The first supervisory responsibility for providing a supportive work environment for teachers is to openly espouse agency values that emphasize individual learning and enjoyment. Supervisors must make it clear in their every day practice that learner skill development and enjoyment is highly valued. Personnel who carry out teaching programs typically have many responsibilities in human service agencies. If supervisors do not place a high priority on ensuring teaching duties are carried out effectively and enjoyably, then other duties will inevitably interfere with fulfilling those duties.

Espousing values that emphasize the importance of teaching involves much more than proclaiming that learning and enjoyment is valued within an agency. Essentially every agency providing teaching services has a mission statement of some kind proclaiming the importance of enhancing independence and enjoyment among its consumer population. Such statements are important, but not sufficient for ensuring a work environment that promotes effective and enjoyable teaching. Supervisors must actively translate mission or value statements into day-to-day action.

The importance of actively placing a priority on teaching is well illustrated through examples of what happens when supervisors do not consistently prioritize teaching services. Common examples include:

- a teacher is required to fill in for an absent staff person and must perform the latter person's duties instead of usual teaching duties
- a learner is not taken to a program site in which teaching occurs because the vehicle used to transport the learner is needed for other purposes
- a supervisor schedules a learner for a haircut or similar appointment at a time when teaching programs normally occur
- a teacher is required to attend a meeting during scheduled teaching times
- a teacher is mandated to spend time completing paper work to prepare for an evaluative survey or review instead of completing teaching duties
- additional learners are temporarily assigned to a teacher due to another staff person's absence such that the teacher cannot realistically complete teaching duties with the teacher's regular learners

Situations such as those just exemplified reflect supervisory practices that fail to effectively prioritize teaching responsibilities. When these situations occur, learners are deprived of opportunities to learn important skills. The practices also are frustrating for teachers, and give teachers the impression that supervisors really do not value teaching. It is a supervisor's responsibility to find ways to resolve the situations without jeopardizing implementation of teaching programs.

Supervisory practices that allow cancellation or prevention of teaching services are especially frustrating for teachers when the supervisors proclaim that learner independence and enjoyment is an agency priority. Such proclamations are apparent in agency documents and brochures, during staff meetings, and in interactions with family members of learners. However, teachers quickly realize supervisors are not sincere in what they proclaim. The result is a work environment that is clearly not supportive of teachers, and seriously impedes the quality of teaching services.

It is incumbent upon supervisors to place a priority on teaching services every day. If supervisors value teaching consumers in their agency, they must find ways to ensure teachers can carry out teaching programs on a regular and consistent basis. In short, supervisors must *actively comply* with the agency's mission of promoting learner independence and enjoyment.

Supervisors can do many things to support teachers in fulfilling an agency's mission of promoting learner skill development and enjoyment. From an organizational perspective, those things generally can be considered within two categories of supervisory actions. The first category pertains to what supervisors can do to facilitate teaching services, or what is often referred to as setting the occasion for effective and enjoyable teaching. The second category pertains to how supervisors should respond to teacher work performance on a daily basis.

Setting The Occasion For Effective And Enjoyable Teaching

Being Knowledgeable About Making Teaching Programs Enjoyable

If supervisors are to effectively support teachers in helping learners enjoy teaching programs, the supervisors must have an awareness of teacher duties necessary for making teaching enjoyable. Supervisors should be familiar with the types of procedures discussed in preceding chapters for enhancing learner enjoyment with teaching programs. Supervisors cannot provide a supportive environment unless they know what to support.

To illustrate, a critical step in making teaching programs enjoyable is for a teacher to establish a good rapport with a learner prior to beginning a teaching program (**Chapter 5**). Establishing a good rapport involves, among other things, a teacher spending time with a learner doing things the learner enjoys. Supervisors need to be aware that spending time with a learner in this manner is a necessary pre-requisite for helping the learner enjoy forthcoming teaching sessions.

If supervisors are not aware of the importance of teachers conducting activities a learner enjoys as part of the relationship-building process, supervisors are likely to wonder why time is spent on those activities. Supervisors may assume the activities are a means for respective teachers to avoid other work duties, and represent wasted work time. If supervisors express these views to teachers, a critical action necessary for teachers to make teaching enjoyable will likely be discouraged. In turn, teachers will experience a lack of support for their teaching duties.

Similar effects of lack of supervisor awareness regarding teacher actions necessary for enhancing learner enjoyment can also occur with other aspects of the teaching process. In particular, when teachers spend time providing preferred activities for a learner immediately after a teaching program (**Chapter 6**), or giving a learner a choice of whether to participate in a teaching program at a given time (**Chapter 7**), supervisors are likely to view such actions as unnecessary. Supervisors subsequently are likely to discourage teachers from engaging in these activities, despite their important role in helping learners enjoy teaching programs.

Teachers should assume some responsibility for informing supervisors about the importance of the types of activities just illustrated. However, the primary responsibility for ensuring supervisory awareness of teacher duties necessary to promote learner enjoyment rests with the supervisors themselves. Supervisors must exert time and effort to become knowledgeable about these important teacher functions. Such knowledge is a necessity for supervisors to actively support teachers in their efforts to make teaching effective and enjoyable for learners.

> **Supervisors cannot effectively support teachers in their efforts to make teaching programs enjoyable unless the supervisors are knowledgeable about the activities in which teachers must engage.**

Practicing Participative Management

One of the best ways for supervisors to set the occasion for effective and enjoyable teaching is to involve teachers in management decisions that affect their teaching duties. Providing teachers opportunities to have input into decisions affecting teaching responsibilities represents a *participative management* approach to supervision; teachers actively participate in the management process.

Participative management strategies have several important benefits. Teacher input in the management process helps supervisors make informed decisions relative to more authoritative supervisory approaches in which supervisors make decisions essentially on their own. Participative management approaches also tend to be well received by teachers. When teachers play an active part in decisions affecting their work routine, their quality of work life and motivation is usually enhanced.

Practicing participative management does not remove ultimate decision-making responsibilities from supervisors. Supervisors continue to have the final authority regarding work duties of their teaching staff, but they attend to the views of staff in applying that authority. Again, this type of supervisory approach typically makes the work environment more supportive from a teacher's perspective.

One area in which teacher input is particularly relevant for supervisors pertains to decisions regarding learner caseloads of teachers. Decisions concerning with whom a teacher works on a day-to-day basis are very important to most teachers, and have a major impact on teacher quality of work life. Teachers may have already established a good relationship with certain learners, and desire to continue working with those learners. Supervisors need to attend to those desires as much as reasonable when considering changes among learner assignments to respective teachers.

In other cases, teachers may experience difficulties in working with certain learners and prefer not to work with those learners if possible. Supervisors likewise should attend to those teacher concerns. In a rather extreme but somewhat common example, some teachers are anxious or even fearful of teaching particular learners due to aggression or other problem behavior the learners display. Supervisors must address such concerns if teachers are to effectively teach the learners, and do so in a way the learners (and teachers) enjoy.

When a teacher is apprehensive about working with a learner, it is a supervisor's responsibility to resolve the teacher's concerns. A supervisor may need to assign the learner to another teacher who is more comfortable with the learner, or provide additional staff resources to help the teacher feel more at ease with the learner. Alternatively, a supervisor may need to seek specialized consultation to help the teacher find ways to address the learner's problem behavior and become more comfortable with the learner.

By employing a participative management approach to supervision, a supervisor is usually well aware of important teacher concerns related to teaching responsibilities. Such awareness sets the occasion for supervisors to resolve the concerns. In turn, supervisors are then taking important steps to make the work environment supportive of teachers and more conducive for effective and enjoyable teaching.

> **Participative management gives teachers input into decisions affecting their teaching duties, and enhances supervisory effectiveness in providing a supportive work environment for teachers.**

Providing Structure For Teacher Work Performance

Another means of setting the occasion for successful teaching performance is for supervisors to provide adequate job structure. Job structure pertains to ensuring that teacher work expectations are very clear. People generally do not enjoy working in conditions in which expectations placed on them are not readily apparent. Supervisors should make sure teachers clearly understand what is expected regarding daily job duties.

Job structure also pertains to providing adequate resources for teachers to fulfill teaching responsibilities in a timely manner. It is very frustrating for teachers when they lack materials for carrying out teaching programs, for example, or they must spent inordinate amounts of time securing necessary materials. Supervisors must know what materials teachers need to complete their duties, and make sure those materials are readily available to teachers when needed. Supervisors should have frequent contact with teachers and actively seek information about what the teachers need to facilitate their teaching duties.

Helping Out

One of the most appreciative actions supervisors can do for teachers is to periodically help the teachers perform aspects of their duties. Teachers sincerely appreciate supervisors who are willing to take time to occasionally help teachers with difficult tasks, or fill in for teachers temporarily when extra time is needed to complete other duties. Of course, the amount of time supervisors help out with teacher duties must be limited such that supervisors can fulfill their other supervisory responsibilities. Nevertheless, every supervisor should be able to help a teacher occasionally. Such efforts can go a long way to making a work environment supportive and motivating for teachers.

Helping out also means that a supervisor actively strives to minimize interference with teaching responsibilities. Numerous expectations can be placed on teachers from time to time that have no bearing on carrying out teaching programs, but can interfere with teacher time devoted to the programs. Often such expectations result from requests or demands of agency executives, or from administrative or regulatory offices.

Whenever possible, supervisors should find ways to help teachers respond to unexpected or unusual job requests without interfering with implementation of teaching programs. Supervisors may be able to seek assistance from other staff to meet the particular demands, complete the duties for teachers themselves, or find ways of avoiding the demands being directed to teachers altogether. Whatever supervisors can do in this respect will not only prevent disruption of teaching duties, but also reduce unpleasantness within teacher work environments. Reducing unpleasantness in the work environment has the overall impact of making the work place more supportive for teachers.

> **When supervisors periodically help teachers with various duties by performing the duties for teachers, a strong sense of support is usually experienced by teachers.**

Promoting Professional Development

Conducting teaching programs that result in learners with developmental disabilities acquiring functional skills in an enjoyable manner is a skillful and effortful undertaking. Every teacher can benefit at times from help in finding ways to more effectively teach a respective learner in a way the learner enjoys. Supervisors can be supportive of teacher efforts in this regard by providing professional opportunities for teachers to advance their knowledge and take advantage of new developments in the teaching field.

Providing professional development opportunities can occur in many ways. Traditional means supervisors have used focus on supporting teachers in attending relevant conferences and seminars, and bringing in experts in the field for presentations and consultations. There are also more day-to-day things supervisors can do to enhance teacher skill development and knowledge.

Supervisors should have sufficient contact with individual teachers to be aware of special problems they encounter in making teaching effective and enjoyable for respective learners. Supervisors should then actively strive to secure information to help teachers overcome the difficulties. Supervisors themselves may know other ways to work with a learner, or be able to obtain relevant literature for a teacher. Supervisors may also be able to find other staff who could help a teacher identify alternative ways to achieve success with a learner.

When supervisors actively support teachers in expanding their professional knowledge and skills, several benefits result. First, learners benefit because teachers become more proficient in carrying out teaching programs in an effective and enjoyable manner. Second, teachers are usually most appreciative of having opportunities to enhance their professional development. Such opportunities help make an overall work environment more enjoyable for teachers, and help teachers maintain motivation for fulfilling their teaching duties.

Supervisors Can Provide A Work Environment For Teachers That Fosters Effective And Enjoyable Teaching By:

Being knowledgeable about what constitutes effective and enjoyable teaching

Practicing participative management

Providing structure for teacher work performance

Helping out

Promoting professional development

Responding In Ways That Support Effective And Enjoyable Teaching

Procedures discussed to this point have focused on what supervisors can do to make it likely that effective and enjoyable teaching will occur on a routine basis. The supervisory procedures are designed to facilitate teacher duties in carrying out teaching responsibilities, and to make attempts to fulfill those duties enjoyable. Another critical part of providing a supportive work environment for teachers is how supervisors *respond* to teacher performance.

Supervisors can enhance the supportive nature of teacher work environments by responding to teaching performances in a manner that shows proficient teaching is valued and appreciated. Receiving favorable acknowledgement from a supervisor for one's work performance can provide a strong sense of support for teachers. In contrast, if supervisors rarely acknowledge teacher performance in carrying out teaching programs, teachers lose or never obtain this major source of support.

Supervisors should find ways to favorably respond to teaching performance on a frequent and regular basis. The most readily available means of responding in this regard is to provide teachers with positive feedback. Positive feedback entails expressing approval about specific aspects of teaching performance.

Positive feedback can be presented in many ways. Expressions of approval for designated areas of teaching performance can be announced in staff meetings, written in formal letters to respective teachers, or presented in informal notes. Frequently though, feedback is best received if supervisors simply tell teachers about commendable aspects of their teaching performances. Supervisors should routinely look for opportunities to verbally commend teachers for their teaching efforts and successes. Although there is no hard and fast rule regarding how often supervisors should provide positive feedback, generally a supervisor should express approval for some aspect of each teacher's performance at least every week.

When supervisors regularly commend teaching performances that pertain to helping learners acquire functional skills in an enjoyable manner, three beneficial outcomes are likely. First, feedback and commendation help teachers maintain their efforts in working diligently to carry out teaching programs. Second, supervisor expressions of approval help teachers feel good about their accomplishments, and represent a source of work-place enjoyment for teachers. Third, and as a direct result of the first two outcomes, learners with disabilities will continue to receive teaching services that promote their skill development and day-to-day enjoyment.

> **Supervisors should provide supportive feedback regarding teaching performance to each teacher at least every week.**

Chapter Review Questions

1. *What is a supervisor's general responsibility in regard to the work environment in which teachers carry out teaching programs?*

2. *What are five general ways a supervisor can set the occasion for providing a supportive work environment for teachers?*

3. *What is participative management and how does it usually affect teacher work motivation?*

4. *What does it mean for a supervisor to provide job structure for teachers?*

5. *What are two beneficial outcomes of a supervisor providing professional development opportunities for teachers?*

6. *What is the most readily available means for a supervisor to respond to teaching performances in a way that provides positive support for teachers?*

7. *At a minimum, how often should supervisors provide positive feedback to teachers for their work performance?*

Section V
Bringing It All Together and Trouble Shooting

Chapter 12

A Checklist For Preference-Based Teaching

Preceding chapters have presented a variety of procedures for building learner enjoyment into teaching programs. Pre-requisite steps that need to be taken prior to initiating a teaching program were described, including using evidence-based teaching practices such as those in the **Teaching Skills Program** in designing the program, selecting functional skills to teach, and developing a good teacher-learner relationship. An overall model for planning a teaching session was then described, focusing on the *Antecedent, Behavior, Consequence (ABC) Model of Preference-Based Teaching*, or what is also known as the *Preferred ABC Model*.

Specific procedures to conduct when applying the *Preferred ABC Model* were also described, including provision of learner choice opportunities as part of the teaching process and providing preferred items and activities. Important considerations regarding the timing of when to conduct teaching sessions were likewise discussed.

When considering all the things that can be done to make teaching programs enjoyable for learners, teachers may begin to feel somewhat overwhelmed with the task. However, in practice, the procedures are not that difficult to apply once a teacher has become familiar with the various practices. Additionally, it is not expected that every individual procedure discussed in preceding chapters will be used with each teaching program or teaching session.

Teachers should decide which preference-based teaching procedures are most relevant to use with a given learner and teaching program. The decisions should be based on what is likely to be most important for a learner's enjoyment as well as what is reasonably practical for the teacher.

In considering which preference-based teaching procedures to focus on when planning and conducting respective teaching programs, there is one procedure that should never be omitted: teachers should always engage activities to develop a good rapport with each learner whom they will teach. good teacher-learner relationship enhances the enjoyment factor associat with essentially every other preference-based procedure. Having a go rapport with a learner is also a powerful means of preventing proble behavior among certain learners that could otherwise occur during teachi sessions.

> **Arguably the most critical factor for making a teaching program enjoyable for a learner with disabilities is the development of a good teacher-learner relationship.**

The Preference-Based Teaching Checklist

To assist in planning and conducting an enjoyable teaching sessic teachers can refer to the *Preference-Based Teaching Checklist* at the end this chapter. The checklist was developed as a tool to help remind teachers the various procedures that can be used to enhance learner enjoyment wi teaching programs. Teachers can quickly review the checklist and check each procedure as they prepare to incorporate it within the teaching proces

The *Preference-Based Teaching Checklist* consists of five parts. The parts pertain to:

- **What should occur when initially considering developing a teaching program for an individual learner**
- **Setting a time and location for eventually conducting a teaching session**
- **What to do immediately before a teaching session**
- **What to do during a teaching session**
- **What to do immediately after a teaching session**

The checklist is designed to be a quick aid for teachers in planni teaching sessions. Additional information regarding each preference-bas procedure provided on the checklist can be obtained by referring to respect chapters that discus each practice in more detail. To facilitate the lat process, the checklist provides the number of each chapter that discusses a given procedure.

Readers can copy the checklist to use in their everyday practice. Alternatively, to obtain a supply of checklist copies, readers can contact the authors (see the **How To Contact The Authors** section in the beginning of the text).

The Preference-Based Teaching Checklist

I. When initially considering developing a teaching program for a learner:
   ___. Spend time developing rapport with the learner (**5***)
       ___. Participate with the learner in activities the learner enjoys (**5**)
       ___. Change the physical and/or social environment to remove features a learner dislikes (**5**)
       ___. Make sure the learner's own communication methods are easily understood (**5**)

II. Set a preferred time and location for the teaching session:
   ___. Do not interrupt an ongoing, highly preferred learner activity (**9**)
   ___. Arrange the session after a period in which the learner has had limited access to preferred items and activities to be used during the session (**9**)
   ___. Identify a preferred learner location for the session (**6**)

III. Immediately before the teaching session:
   ___. Engage the learner in a brief preferred activity (**6, 8**)
   ___. Provide at least one choice to the learner about some aspect of how the teaching session will proceed (**7**)

IV. During the teaching session:
   ___. Provide brief, preferred activities between some instructional trials (**6**)
   ___. Provide a brief break and preferred activity following any sign of learner discontent, followed immediately with a return to the part of the instructional trial where the break occurred (**6**)

V. Immediately after the teaching session:
   ___. Provide a choice regarding a preferred activity in which the learner can engage (**7**)
   ___. Make sure a *highly preferred* activity is available for the learner (**6, 8**)

* Numbers in parentheses ( ) refer to chapters discussing the identified procedures.

Chapter 13
Frequently Asked Questions About
Preference-Based Teaching

As with any approach to teaching people who have developmental disabilities, questions are likely to arise as teachers begin to practice preference-based teaching with individual learners. This chapter presents the most frequently asked questions that have arisen when teachers use this approach to help individuals with developmental disabilities enjoy learning. The questions have been raised by colleagues with whom we have worked over the years in various teaching settings.

We have attempted to respond to each question in a manner based on our work in developing and applying specific aspects of preference-based teaching. Additionally, we have attempted to respond to each question in regard to what existing behavior analytic research would suggest is the most appropriate response based on the evidence to date. We hope the questions and our responses will be beneficial for teachers who use preference-based teaching to help individuals with developmental disabilities enjoy learning new and meaningful skills.

Does preference-based teaching require more time for carrying out a teaching program than traditional ways of implementing teaching programs?

Incorporating preference-based teaching procedures into teaching sessions does require more time than usual ways in which teaching programs are carried out. Each component of the *Preferred Antecedent, Behavior, Consequence (ABC) Model* adds time to the teaching process. Depending on how many specific procedures are used within the *A*, *B*, and *C* components, the amount of extra time may range from a few minutes to as much as 20 minutes or so. It also takes time for a teacher to establish a good relationship with a learner prior to beginning a program using preference-based teaching. Generally, we have found that if procedures for establishing rapport with a learner are conducted consistently as described in **Chapter 5**, appropriate rapport can usually be established in about one week.

Isn't it better to teach people with developmental disabilities in typical community environments during naturally occurring activities instead of formal teaching sessions in classrooms and other noncommunity settings as represented in this book?

Teaching in natural community settings is very important (see discussion on *naturalistic teaching* in **Chapter 10**). However, there is ample research to show that learners with even the most significant disabilities can learn meaningful skills in formal teaching sessions in classrooms and related settings that are distinct from the environments in which the skills being taught would be used. Research suggests that for maximum benefits in terms of learners acquiring new skills and being able to use those skills in appropriate situations in typical environments, teaching should occur in both formal sessions and in typical communities. The approaches we have found most beneficial are: (1) begin the teaching process with formal teaching sessions and then add naturalistic teaching procedures as the learners begin to master the skills being taught or when possible, (2) carry out both types of teaching approaches simultaneously during different times of the week.

The part of preference-based teaching that indicates learner discontent, or what may be considered problem behavior during teaching, should be followed by a break from teaching and a preferred activity seems to contradict what learning principles and behavioral research have shown. Won't this strategy reinforce such behavior by allowing learners to escape or avoid part of the teaching that they do not like?

We have been concerned about this issue as well. However, our research and experience have indicated that learner behavior suggesting discontent with part of the teaching will not increase by using these specific procedures, and usually decreases. The reason for the latter results seems to be due to one or more of the following factors. First, by using multiple strategies to make teaching programs more enjoyable for learners, the negative aspect of the programs likely are reduced such that learner discontent or problem behavior is less likely to occur. Second, it is important to remember (see discussion in **Chapter 6**) that after the break and brief preferred activity is provided following signs of learner discontent, the teacher always returns to the point in the instructional process at which the break occurred and then prompts the learner through the remaining part in the process. Hence, the learner does not really escape or avoid part of the teaching process following indices of discontent, the learner just receives a short interruption with the process. We believe that always returning to the point at which the break was initiated and then prompting the learner through the process is critical to avoid inadvertently reinforcing problem behavior. Nonetheless, if data suggest that discontent or related problem behavior does not decrease or increases, this part of preference-based teaching should probably be discontinued. Other components of the *Preferred ABC Model* should then be relied on to make the teaching program enjoyable for the learner.

What if I am able to help a learner enjoy a teaching program but the learner is still not making progress with the program?

This can happen. Generally it means the right teaching procedures are not being used (e.g., the type of prompting, what is used as a reinforcer for responses to trials), or not being used in the right manner. If, after a teacher has reviewed how the teaching is being done and is pretty confident appropriate procedures are being used in the right manner, then we have found the following steps to usually result in increased progress on a teaching program. First, consider implementing the program more often during the week, such as two or three times per day. We have found that a lot of programs are carried out too infrequently to help a learner acquire the targeted skills, and simply increasing how often the program is taught will bring about progress. Second, have several people who have experience with teaching come observe a few of the teaching sessions and then offer procedural suggestions. The people do not have to be national experts, just other support persons who carry out teaching programs but have not been involved with the program of concern. A lot of times, people who are not involved in a program can see some things that might be changed to help the program's effectiveness.

I have many teaching programs to carry out with different students. Won't preference-based teaching become overly cumbersome and time consuming if I use the approach with all program?

If preference-based teaching is applied with all procedural aspects, it can add to the time and effort in carrying out many programs with one learner or with different learners. However, in many cases, the amount of time to implement a given program decreases because the learner tends to be more responsive to the teaching. Nevertheless, if there are significant time limitations that can't be altered, the following considerations may help. First, use preference-based teaching in its entirety with a program that seems to be most disliked by a learner. Second, across various programs, include only aspects of the *Preferred ABC Model* that are likely to be most enjoyed by a learner. Third, priority should be given to spending time with each learner to establish a very good rapport with the learner. When this happens, teacher praise often becomes highly preferred by the learner and functions as a potent reinforcer. Praise can then be used with every program to enhance its enjoyment capacity for the learner, and providing praise requires minimal teacher time and effort.

Will using preference-based procedures detract from a student developing a "love of learning"?

First of all, a "love of learning" means different things to different people. Nonetheless, procedures constituting preference-based teaching will not detract from a person with developmental disabilities wanting to learn more. Actually, it is highly likely that as a learner participates in programs that are carried out in accordance with preference-based teaching procedures, the learner will increase his or her desire to participate in future teaching programs.

Section VI

Selected Readings and Appendices

Selected Readings

Person-Centered Supports

Browder, D. M., Bambara, L. M., & Belfiore, P. J. (1997). Using a person-centered approach in community-based instruction for adults with developmental disabilities. *Journal of Behavioral Education, 7,* 519-528.

Everson, J. M., & Reid, D. H. (1997). Using person-centered planning to determine employment preferences among people with the most severe disabilities. *Journal of Vocational Rehabilitation, 9,* 99-108.

Everson, J. M., & Reid, D. H. (1999). *Person-centered planning and outcome management: Maximizing organizational effectiveness in supporting quality lifestyles among people with disabilities.* Morganton, NC: Habilitative Management Consultants.

Holburn, S. (1997). A renaissance in residential behavior analysis? A historical perspective and a better way to help people with challenging behavior. *The Behavior Analyst, 20,* 61-85.

Holburn, S. (2002). How science can evaluate and enhance person-centered planning. *Research & Practice for Persons with Severe Disabilities, 27,* 250-260.

Holburn, S., & Vietze, P. (2002). *Person-centered planning: Research, practice, and future directions.* Baltimore: Brookes Publishing.

Hulgin, K. M. (2004). Person-centered services and organizational context: Taking stock of working conditions and their impact. *Mental Retardation, 42,* 169-180.

Minor, C. A., & Bates, P. E. (1997). The effect of person-centered planning activities on the IEP/transition planning process. *Education and Training in Mental Retardation and Developmental Disabilities, 32,* 105-112.

Mount, B. (1997). *Person-centered planning: Finding directions for change using personal futures planning.* New York: Graphic Futures.

O'Brien, J., & O'Brien, C. L. (2002). *Implementing person-centered planning: Voices of experience.* Toronto: Inclusion Press.

Providing Choice Opportunities for People with Developmental Disabilities

Bambara, L. M., Koger, F., Katzer, T., & Davenport, T. A. (1995). Embedding choice in the context of daily routines: An experimental case study. *Journal of The Association for Persons with Severe Handicaps, 20,* 185-195.

Belfiore, P. J., Toro-Zambrana, W. (1994). *Recognizing choices in community settings by people with significant disabilities.* Washington, D.C.: American Association on Mental Retardation.

Cooper, K. J., & Browder, D. M. (1998). Enhancing choice and participation for adults with severe disabilities in community-based instruction. *Journal of The Association for Persons with Severe Handicaps, 23,* 252-260.

Cooper, K. J., & Browder, D. M. (2001). Preparing staff to enhance participation of adults with severe disabilities by offering choice and prompting performance during a community purchase activity. *Research in Developmental Disabilities, 22,* 1-20.

Lancioni, G. E., O'Reilly, M. G., & Emerson, E. (1996). A review of choice research with people with severe and profound developmental disabilities. *Research in Developmental Disabilities, 17,* 391-411.

Parsons, M. B., Harper, V. N., Jensen, J. M., & Reid, D. H. (1997). Assisting older adults with severe disabilities in expressing leisure preferences: A protocol for determining choice-making skills. *Research in Developmental Disabilities, 18,* 113-126.

Parsons, M. B., McCarn, J. E., & Reid, D. H. (1993). Evaluating and increasing meal-related choices throughout a service setting for people with severe disabilities. *Journal of The Association for Persons with Severe Handicaps, 18,* 253-260.

Parsons, M. B., & Reid, D. H. (1990). Assessing food preferences among persons with profound mental retardation: Providing opportunities to make choices. *Journal of Applied Behavior Analysis, 23,* 183-195.

Reid, D. H., & Parsons, M. B. (1991). Making choice a routine part of mealtimes for persons with profound mental retardation. *Behavioral Residential Treatment, 6,* 249-261.

Salmento, M., & Bambara, L. M. (2000). Teaching staff members to provide choice opportunities for adults with multiple disabilities. *Journal of Positive Behavior Interventions, 2,* 12-21.

Sigafoos, J., & Dempsey, R. (1992). Assessing choice making among children with multiple disabilities. *Journal of Applied Behavior Analysis, 25,* 747-755.

Systematic Preference Assessments for Determining Preferred Items and Activities Among People with Developmental Disabilities

Carr, J. E., Nicolson, A. C., & Higbee, T. S. (2000). Evaluation of a brief multiple-stimulus preference assessment in a naturalistic context. *Journal of Applied Behavior Analysis, 33,* 353-357.

Foxx, R. M., Faw, G. D., Taylor, S., Davis, P. K., & Fulia, R. (1993). "Would I be able to . . . "? Teaching clients to assess the availability of their community living life style preferences. *American Journal on Mental Retardation, 98,* 235-248.

Green, C. W., Reid, D. H., Canipe, V. S., & Gardner, S. M. (1991). A comprehensive evaluation of reinforcer identification processes for persons with profound multiple handicaps. *Journal of Applied Behavior Analysis, 24,* 537-552.

Hughes, C., Pitkin, S. E., & Lorden, S. W. (1998). Assessing preferences and choices of persons with severe and profound mental retardation. *Education and Training in Mental Retardation and Developmental Disabilities, 33,* 299-316.

Ivancic, M. T. (2000). Stimulus preference and reinforcer assessment applications. In J. Austin & J. E. Carr (Eds.), *Handbook of applied behavior analysis* (pp. 19-38). Reno, NV: Context Press.

Lattimore, L. P., Parsons, M. B., & Reid, D. H. (2002). A prework assessment of task preferences among adults with autism beginning a supported job. *Journal of Applied Behavior Analysis, 35,* 85-88.

Lattimore, L. P., Parsons, M. B., & Reid, D. H. (2003). Assessing preferred work among adults with autism beginning supported jobs: Identification of constant and alternating task preferences. *Behavioral Interventions, 18,* 161-177.

Lohrmann-O'Rourke, S., & Browder, D. M. (1998). Empirically based methods to assess the preferences of individuals with severe disabilities. *American Journal on Mental Retardation, 103,* 146-161.

Lohrmann-O'Rourke, S., Browder, D. M., & Brown, F. (2000). Guidelines for conducting socially valid systematic preference assessments. *Journal of The Association for Persons with Severe Handicaps, 25,* 42-53.

Newton, J. S., Ard, W. R., & Horner, R. H. (1993). Validating predicted activity preferences of individuals with severe disabilities. *Journal of Applied Behavior Analysis, 26,* 239-245.

Parsons, M. B., Reid, D. H., & Green, C. W. (2001). Situational assessment of task preferences among adults with multiple severe disabilities in supported work. *Journal of The Association for Persons with Severe Handicaps, 26,* 50-55.

Reid, D. H., DiCarlo, C. F., Schepis, M. M., Hawkins, J., & Stricklin, S. B. (2003). Observational assessment of toy preferences among young children with disabilities in inclusive settings: Efficiency analysis and comparison with staff opinion. *Behavior Modification, 27,* 233-250.

Reid, D. H., Everson, J. M., & Green, C. W. (1999). A systematic evaluation of preferences identified through person-centered planning for people with profound multiple disabilities. *Journal of Applied Behavior Analysis, 32,* 467-477.

Reid, D. H., Parsons, M. B., & Green, C. W. (1998). Identifying work preferences among individuals with severe multiple disabilities prior to beginning supported work. *Journal of Applied Behavior Analysis, 31,* 281-285.

Roane, H. S., Vollmer, T. R., Ringdahl, J. E., & Marcus, B. A. (1998). Evaluation of a brief stimulus preference assessment. *Journal of Applied Behavior Analysis, 31,* 605-620.

Naturalistic Teaching Procedures

Charlop-Christy, M. H., & Carpenter, M. H. (2000). Modified incidental teaching sessions: A procedure for parents to increase spontaneous speech in their children with autism. *Journal of Positive Behavior Interventions, 2,* 98-112.

Haring, T. G., Neetz, J. A., Lovinger, L., Peck, C., & Semmel, M. I. (1987). Effects of four modified incidental teaching procedures to create opportunities for communication. *Journal of The Association for Persons with Severe Handicaps, 12,* 218-226.

Hart, B., & Risley, T. R. (1975). Incidental teaching of language in the preschool. *Journal of Applied Behavior Analysis, 8,* 411-420.

Hart, B. M., & Risley, T. R. (1982). *How to use incidental teaching for elaborating language.* Lawrence, KS: H & H Enterprises.

McGee, G. G., Krantz, P. J., Mason, D., & McClannahan, L. E. (1983). A modified incidental-teaching procedure for autistic youth: Acquisition and generalization of receptive object labels. *Journal of Applied Behavior Analysis, 16,* 329-338.

McGee, G. G., Krantz, P. J., & McClannahan, L. E. (1985). The facilitative effects of incidental teaching on preposition use by autistic children. *Journal of Applied Behavior Analysis, 18,* 17-31.

McGee, G. G., Morrier, M. J., & Daly, T. (1999). An incidental teaching approach to early intervention for toddlers with autism. *Journal of the Association for Persons with Severe Handicaps, 24,* 133-146.

Schepis, M. M., Reid, D. H., Behrmann, M. M., & Sutton, K. A. (1998). Increasing communicative interactions of young children with autism using a voice output communication aid and naturalistic teaching. *Journal of Applied Behavior Analysis, 31,* 561-578.

Schepis, M. M., Reid, D. H., Ownbey, J., & Parsons, M. B. (2001).Training support staff to embed teaching within natural routines of young children with disabilities in an inclusive preschool. *Journal of Applied Behavior Analysis, 34,* 313-327.

Venn, M. L., Wolery, M., Werts, M. G., Morris, A., DeCesare, L. D., & Cuffs, M. S. (1993). Embedded instruction in art activities to teach preschoolers with disabilities to imitate their peers. *Early Childhood Research Quarterly, 8,* 277-294.

Wolery, M., Anthony, L., Snyder, E. D., Werts, M. G., & Katzenmeyer, J. (1997). Training elementary teachers to embed instruction during classroom activities. *Education and Treatment of Children, 20,* 40-58.

Appendix A

Research Investigations That Developed And Validated Procedures Used In *Preference-Based Teaching*

Belfiore, P. J., Browder, D. M., & Mace, F. C. (1993). Effects of community and center-based settings on the alertness of persons with profound mental retardation. *Journal of Applied Behavior Analysis, 26,* 401-402.

Carr, E. G., Newsom, C. D., & Binkoff, J. A. (1980). Escape as a factor in the aggressive behavior of two retarded children. *Journal of Applied Behavior Analysis, 13,* 101-117.

Dunlap, G., Foster-Johnson, L., Clarke, S., Kern, L., & Childs, K. E. (1995). Modifying activities to produce functional outcomes: Effects on the problem behaviors of students with disabilities. *Journal of The Association for Persons with Severe Handicaps, 20,* 248-258.

Dunlap, G., Kern-Dunlap, L., Clarke, S., & Robbins, F. R. (1991). Functional assessment, curricular revision, and severe behavior problems. *Journal of Applied Behavior Analysis, 24,* 387-397.

Dunlap, G., & Koegel, R. L. (1980). Motivating autistic children through stimulus variation. *Journal of Applied Behavior Analysis, 13,* 619-627.

Dyer, K. (1989). The effects of preference on spontaneous verbal requests in individuals with autism. *Journal of The Association for Person with Severe Handicaps, 14,* 184-189.

Dyer, K., Dunlap, G., & Winterling, V. (1990). Effects of choice making on the serious problem behaviors of students with severe handicaps. *Journal of Applied Behavior Analysis, 23,* 515-524.

Ebanks, M. E., & Fisher, W. W. (2003). Altering the timing of academic prompts to treat destructive behavior maintained by escape. *Journal of Applied Behavior Analysis, 36,* 355-359.

Foster-Johnson, L., Ferro, J., & Dunlap, G. (1994). Preferred curricular activities and reduced problem behaviors in students with intellectual disabilities. *Journal of Applied Behavior Analysis, 27,* 493-504.

Gottschalk, J. M., Libby, M. E., & Graff, R. B. (2000). The effects of establishing operations on preference assessment outcomes. *Journal of Applied Behavior Analysis, 33,* 85-88.

Green, C. W., Gardner, S. M., Canipe, V. S., & Reid, D. H. (1994). Analyzing alertness among people with profound multiple disabilities: Implications for provision of training. *Journal of Applied Behavior Analysis, 27,* 519-531.

Green, C. W., Gardner, S. M., & Reid, D. H. (1997). Increasing indices of happiness among people with profound multiple disabilities: A program replication and component analysis. *Journal of Applied Behavior Analysis, 30,* 217-228.

Green, C. W., & Reid, D. H. (1996). Defining, validating, and increasing indices of happiness among people with profound multiple disabilities. *Journal of Applied Behavior Analysis, 29,* 67-78.

Green, C. W., & Reid, D. H. (1999). Reducing indices of unhappiness among individuals with profound multiple disabilities during therapeutic exercise routines. *Journal of Applied Behavior Analysis, 32,* 137-148.

Green, C. W., & Reid, D. H. (1999). A behavioral approach to identifying sources of happiness and unhappiness among individuals with profound multiple disabilities. *Behavior Modification, 23,* 280-293.

Horner, R. H., Day, H. M., Sprague, J. R., O'Brien, M., & Heathfield, L. T. (1991). Interspersed requests: A nonaversive procedure for reducing aggression and self-injury during instruction. *Journal of Applied Behavior Analysis, 24,* 265-278.

Ivancic, M. T., Barrett, G. T., Simonow, A., & Kimberly, A. (1997). A replication to increase happiness indices among some people with profound multiple disabilities. *Research in Developmental Disabilities, 18,* 79-89.

Kern, L., Vorndran, C. M., Hilt, A., Ringdahl, J. E., Adelman, B. E., & Dunlap, G. (1998). Choice as an intervention to improve behavior: A review of the literature. *Journal of Behavioral Education, 8,* 151-169.

Klatt, K. P., Sherman, J. A., & Sheldon, J. B. (2000). Effects of deprivation on engagement in preferred activities by persons with developmental disabilities. *Journal of Applied Behavior Analysis, 33,* 495-506.

Logan, K. R., Jacobs, H. A., Gast, D. L., Murray, A. S., Daino, K., & Skala, C. (1998). The impact of typical peers on the perceived happiness of students with profound multiple disabilities. *Journal of The Association for Persons with Severe Handicaps, 23,* 309-318.

Mace, A. B., Shapiro, E. S., & Mace, F. C. (1998). Effects of warning stimuli for reinforcer withdrawal and task onset on self-injury. *Journal of Applied Behavior Analysis, 31,* 679-682.

Moes, D. R. (1998). Integrating choice-making opportunities within teacher-assigned academic tasks to facilitate the performance of children with autism. *Journal of The Association for Persons with Severe Handicaps, 23,* 319-328.

Romaniuk, C., Miltenberger, R., Conyers, C., Jenner, N., Jurgens, M., & Ringenberg, C. (2002). The influence of activity choice on problem behaviors maintained by escape versus attention. *Journal of Applied Behavior Analysis, 35,* 349-362.

Seybert, S., Dunlap, G., & Ferro, J. (1996). The effects of choice-making on the problem behaviors of high school students with intellectual disabilities. *Journal of Behavioral Education, 6,* 49-65.

Umbreit, J., & Blair, K. (1996). The effects of preference, choice, and attention on problem behavior at school. *Education and Training in Mental Retardation and Developmental Disabilities, 31,* 151-161.

Vaughn, B. J., & Horner, R. H. (1997). Identifying instructional tasks that occasion problem behaviors and assessing the effects of student versus teacher choice among these tasks. *Journal of Applied Behavior Analysis, 30,* 299-312.

Appendix B

The Teaching Skills Program

Detailed information on the **Teaching Skills Program** is provided in the *Instructor's Manual* for ***Training To Teach In A Day: The Teaching-Skills Training Program (2nd Printing)***. The manual provides in-depth description of four essential teaching skills: (1) following a task analysis, (2) using a least-to-most assistive prompt sequence, (3) correcting learner errors and, (4) reinforcing learner progress. Special manual features include:

- **Step-by-step instructions for training people to teach**
- **Sample task analyses of teaching programs**
- **Observation procedures and form for diagnosing teaching accuracy and mistakes**
- **Mastery tests to assess knowledge of the teaching skills**

The manual is available for $23.00 plus $2.00 shipping from the Carolina Behavior Analysis and Support Center, Ltd., P. O. Box 425, Morganton, NC 28680 (phone: 828 432 0030; fax 828 433 8889; e-mail drhmc@vistatech.net). The manual can also be purchased by copying and mailing or faxing the ordering form below.

ORDERING FORM FOR THE INSTRUCTOR'S *MANUAL FOR TRAINING TO TEACH IN A DAY: THE TEACHING-SKILLS TRAINING PROGRAM* **(2ND PRINTING)**

NUMBER OF MANUALS ORDERED: _____

TOTAL ORDER AMOUNT ENCLOSED: $_____

PURCHASE ORDER # (if available): _____

Manual should be sent to:

NAME: _____

ADDRESS: _____

_____

Appendix C
Instructions for Evaluating and Completing The Checklist for Teaching Proficiency

1) Were steps taught in the proper order as listed in the task analysis?

Score "yes" if the steps were taught in the order as written in the task analysis.

Score "no" if any of the steps were taught out of the written order.

Score "NA" (non applicable) if there is no written task analysis for the skill, the skill involved only one step, or order did not matter.

2) Were all prompts appropriate?

Score "yes" if more than one prompt was needed on a given step in the task analysis and if each prompt provided for the step was more helpful than the preceding prompt.

Score "no" if prompts were repeated for a step, a second prompt was needed for a step but the second prompt was not more helpful than the first prompt, or if full physical guidance was used as the first prompt for any step.

Score "NA" if no more than one prompt was needed on all steps.

3) Were all error corrections provided appropriately?

Score "yes" if for each error that occurred, the step was repeated where the error occurred and more help was provided on the learner's second attempt to complete the step *and* sufficient help was provided such that the learner correctly completed the step on the second attempt.

Score "no" if the learner made an error and the error was ignored, or the learner made the same error on a step on the second attempt.

Score "NA" if the learner made no errors on any step.

4) Was a reinforcing consequence provided following the last step?

Score "yes" if a positive consequence was provided following the last step in the task analysis completed by the learner.

Score "no" if no positive consequence was provided following the last step in the task analysis completed by the learner.

Index

age appropriate 49-52
aggression 4, 16, 53, 73, 86, 121, 134, 135, 150
alertness 118, 119, 127
antecedents 75, 76-81, 92, 98, 99, 115
applied behavior analysis 4, 15, 120, 163
apprehension 71, 73, 150
augmentative communication 95
autism 7, 125, 126
Asperger's Syndrome 126
caseloads 150
challenging behavior (see problem behavior)
choice 51, 52, 91-103, 122-123, 149, 159, 162
communication 53-54, 63, 69-71, 93, 95, 103, 110, 136, 162
compliance 39-41
consequences 75, 88-90, 92, 98, 102-103, 115
control 3, 4, 40, 92, 101, 123, 138, 139, 141
discontent (of learners) 4-5, 8, 16, 17, 40, 61, 68-69, 83-88, 121-122, 126, 134, 162, 165
embedded teaching 135
error correction 29, 35-37, 61
evidence-based practices 9-10, 15-20, 26, 38, 118-120, 128-129, 134, 159
familiarity (with learners) 62, 63, 64, 93, 95, 103, 110, 111
fear 71, 73, 150
Federal Title XIX Medicaid Program 17
feedback 154-155
formal teaching programs 8-9
free access observation 111-113
functional skills 3, 10, 43-55, 59, 152, 154, 159, 164
incidental teaching 135-136
Individual Education Plans 9, 25
Individual Family Service Plans 9
Individual Habilitative Plans 9, 25
Individual Program Plans 9, 125
Intermediate Care Facilities 17
interspersing (teaching tasks) 84
job structure 150, 152
least-to-most helpful prompting (see also prompting) 34-35, 87, 136
leisure 49-52
meaningful skills (see functional skills)
mild disabilities 7
modeling 143
motivation (of teachers) 138-144, 145, 149, 151, 153

naturalistic teaching 9, 135-138, 142, 164
paired-item choice 93-97, 113
participative management 149-150, 153
person-centered 54-55
person-centered plans 9
preference assessment 108-115
Preferred Antecedent, Behavior, Consequence (ABC) Model 75-90, 107, 115, 159, 164, 165, 166
problem behavior 3, 4, 16, 52-54, 63, 65, 98, 121-122, 134-135, 150, 164-165
professional development 152-153
profound disabilities 7, 28
profound multiple disabilities 26
prompting 5, 8, 28, 32-35, 61, 137
property destruction 4, 16, 73, 134
quality of life 17, 91, 108
rapport (teacher-learner) 62-74, 77, 106, 148, 160, 162, 166
reinforcement 29, 37-39, 89, 105-106, 140-144
relationships (teacher-learner) 11, 59-73, 93, 122, 148, 150, 159, 160
resistance (to teaching) 4, 16-17, 66, 76
self-motivation (of teachers) 138-144
self-help skills 4, 46-47
self-injury 4, 16, 73, 86, 126
self-recording 140
self-reinforcement 35, 140-144
severe disabilities (description of) 7-8
sign language 53, 70, 136
signals (of forthcoming change) 81, 122, 126
state conditions 127-129
supervision 139, 143-148, 145-155
supervisors 11, 72-73, 138, 139, 143-144, 145-155
systematic preference assessment 114-115
task analysis 9, 29-32, 33, 82, 89, 106, 135, 137
teaching trials 76, 80, 81, 82-85, 87, 88, 105, 106, 107, 127, 128, 136, 137, 162
teaching proficiency 38-39, 145, 153, 154
Teaching Skills Program 26-39
technology (of teaching) 4, 5, 15, 28
values 146-148, 153
vocational skills 48-49, 102
voice output communication 70
work performance (of teachers) 143-144, 145
work readiness 48